D

First Edition, 2008
All rights reserved

Library of Congress Cataloging-in-Publication Data

Dragomoshchenko, A. (Arkadii)
Dust / Arkadii Dragomoshchenko ; translations by Evgeny Pavlov ...
[et al.]. -- 1st ed.
    p. cm.
ISBN 978-1-56478-419-3 (pbk. : alk. paper)
I. Pavlov, Evgeny, 1968- II. Title.
PG3479.6.R28D87 2008
891.78'44--dc22

                    2008017381

"Do Not a Gun" was first published in *Amerika: Russian Writers View the United
States*, edited by Mikhail Iossel and Jeff Parker (Dalkey Archive Press, 2004);
"Here" was first published in New Zealand, in the literary magazine *Sport* (no. 28,
Autumn 2002); "Light" appeared in *Crossing Centuries: The New Generations in
Russian Poetry*, edited by John High et al. (Jersey City: Talisman House, 2000).

Partially funded by a grant from the Illinois Arts Council, a state agency, and by
the University of Illinois at Urbana-Champaign

www.dalkeyarchive.com

Printed on permanent/durable acid-free paper and bound
in the United States of America

DUST

ARKADII DRAGOMOSHCHENKO

TRANSLATIONS FROM THE RUSSIAN BY EVGENY PAVLOV,
THOMAS EPSTEIN, SHUSHAN AVAGYAN, AND ANA LUCIC

DALKEY ARCHIVE PRESS
CHAMPAIGN AND LONDON

BLACK OPEN-BACKED EVENING DRESS 1

FINCHES 13

HERE 19

PETERSBURG IN THE MARGINS 40

DO NOT A GUN 48

SAND TO SAND 78

LIGHT 89

DUST 91

former and the latter are impossible? I turn around the corner and see a brick wall, red-hot from the midday sun.

The birds in the distance play with their flowing reflections in the air. Can you hear my voice? Close your eyes, hold your breath, and repeat that sentence about the birds. *What*—quick now—*are you imagining*? Nothing. So, if we take out that sentence, will anything change? Probably not. Nothing will change. Nothing at all . . . But I want that sentence there because, as I read it out loud, I start remembering myself repeating those words for the very first time in that exact order. Their traces flicker behind the window. While the traces left by a hot cup that's been sitting by my monitor are gradually vanishing. I'll come clean: I just brought the cup of coffee to my mouth. He's about to write, "My walks have gotten longer," in a letter to an acquaintance whose name won't be revealed. Introducing a character, then—or why not four. Then eliminating some in turn. We choose our paper, touch the impassive margins of anticipation with a sharp pencil. From this point on, he writes, the day will begin from the Petrograd Side.

Walking around the Peter and Paul Fortress, coming from the Artillery Museum, I leave behind—it hasn't happened yet, but I will write about it nonetheless, gradually actualizing the movement past the aforementioned landmarks in my particular, ethereal stream-of-consciousness manner of writing "from memory"—the mosque, and as I continue walking, the back of my head feels the combination of the two azures, sky and cupola, behind me, with raised inscriptions and sparsely scattered clouds.

She is surprised to see a stranger appear from around the corner, like a raster image formed from the trembling of a sail on the surface of her pupil. Their gazes meet for a split second. A gray whirlwind of dust rises up to the sky. Further along we have Pushkin House, the Stock Exchange, North Beach, Embarcadero, St. Nicholas Bridge, Telegraph Street—all those places that you know so well.

I'll come to you in the morning. I'll pass through the gates of architectural phantoms, enter your room, brush aside the golden shroud of wasps with my hand, wipe the sweat from your face, Nina, and no one will be able to tear me away from you—no one! And when the sun sets, we'll lie on the floor like two handfuls of ashes and turn into little useless objects, like blue poppy petals in the celluloid sphere of a watch. Shreds of torn paper, the slanting wind in your face, wasps, a cadenced sound in your ears. When you'll become transparent to yourself. Not a single affirmation. An effortless walk through nonexistence. Just a few more patient strokes, and it would be possible to start talking about the structure and logic of its secret interrelations.

For example, why was I standing in front of a brick wall that morning? There was a hill behind me and little figurines made of heat kept falling on me, for an infinitely long time. The sun wasn't scorching, but still my eyes hurt, as though I'd been up watching how drops of blood coagulate on glass all night long. I made out a faint silhouette on my left.

The device of the imagination presupposes a constant projection of the past onto the future, with a simultaneous change reflected in the experiences produced by the "past." The final change is conventional, too. She stood peering into the unsteady radiance playing on the asphalt, then turned around. The edges of her black silk jacket fluttered in the wind. Ice and yellow light were standing around like the last numbers of some forgotten theorem, smoldering in lilac hues where her silk outline ended. What was she wearing, among so many overexposed objects and names? The light is in the way. A dialogue follows. Instructions: get a handful of dirt, mix it with hellebore, pour the concoction under your feet—a lesson for the ear—slowly, drop by drop. What happens in the head is much more interesting. The quiet, midday stupor of attics; lilacs in the garden; bumblebees frozen trembling inside peonies; a rustle of unrecognized, untraceable speech; faces against the sun—the same faces: they get near you and at the last moment slip away with the movements of their fingers, in an effort to explain, pointing towards the aging of some news receding now into the silver-tree crowns, and only a quick knife, reflected by the memory of spring creeks, can painlessly separate the hidden darkness of summer into a touch that wants nothing in return, and a string of lightning. A broken glass. Vertigo.

Try something else, find a different approach, start with the steppe. I recall we ended our conversation saying that from a certain moment on one stops depending on anything. *What* are we to others when we're in each other's arms? *What* belongs to whom? We turn into co-owners of the same items—the same skin, same breath, same blood cells, with the same inexpressibly short-term memory, coiled in unseen hurricanes and sandstorms. Frozen steps in family albums.

Perhaps this was expected; it's also possible that we were trying to make it happen; it can't be ruled out that such expectations make up a part of the sum of meanings that form our lives. Though this is hard to believe. I won't even try to. Why should I?

But I'm honest when I write to you because today I'm utterly convinced that all my words are devoid of thought and exist only as ghosts appearing at certain moments of weakness, working in optical shifts, when the phases of the moon coincide and release vapors that gently change the optics of round mirrors. I'm just waiting—it'll be an illumination, a reward, an inexplicable rupture—for nothing that I actually expect to happen. Before, at this point, I always used to talk about the act of falling as a drastic change of proportions and scale. Motives are important. My fingernails shine, and each reflects a cloud, and each cloud hides a bird, and each bird has a ruby cherry in its beak. The fans are folded. A cinnabar moth keeps searching for dreams on the glass. There's a creaking. Each cell is a well from which an utterance draws its wholeness.

They draw it from one's desires, too. In this case, it would be more reasonable to talk not about one's dependence on a certain language or discourse, but about a feeling of impulsive non-complacency. Time not only alters the skin on your face and hands, but also the membrane around any one of your intentions, so to speak—even if these sometimes arrive wearing an additional layer of vague muttering. By which I imply that I have a slight attraction to any manifestation of the world outside "myself."

I only have a few dozen words left at my disposal. What will my narrative be like when I've exhausted them as well? Besides, what seemed at one point like an inexhaustible means of discovering reality, which was rushing towards you from everywhere, expecting your body's full participation (or so you liked to think)—has now changed its configuration, turning, say, into something convex, scattering quickly, and quickly disappearing.

He sat down on a bench in the square on Stremyannaya Street. Call me Aleksandr. The sun flickered a few times through the branches; its heavy rays fell halfway but didn't reach the moist ground, breaking up into wet flares in the air. "What were you dreaming, Aleksandr?" "I dreamt of vowels forcing their way into my name, and how they changed the essence of every single consonant."

Quiet engravings, coin machines, the flutter of two dried wings. The air was permeated with a smell of burning rubber. The kids were burning garbage that summer with a frantic consistency. The young woman sitting at the other end of the bench was saying, "Imagine what a woman feels like when she's in bed next to you, Aleksandr, with this stench coming in from the window . . ." The light broke up along the hillside, chariots moved across the sky with a speed that echoed under the skin with a lingering, minty numbness. The woman by the wall took a step and then hesitated. At noon, the rays, like shrieking gulls, shifted to the other side of the bridge. I remembered my dream.

Dreams move across the body like convoys traveling to destinations known only to them. Until you tell me why you decided to stay here with me, *Get out!* This dream used to mean so much to me. Yet none of the words remaining to me are capable of assuming the form of even the most insignificant detail of this dream, which would nonetheless be of great importance to me—those details that make up the fabric of a dream—and retaining it in my consciousness until I have other dreams that will tell me whether these words are mine or someone else's. These words cast shadows, like those that originate from similar words and thus generate new terms, or like dogs running by a brick wall, their velvet tongues hanging out.

Don't forget that you owe me thirty thousand rubles—though by the time this story appears in print, "thirty thousand" will be a different number (a different value?). Does this apply to other elements of my speech as well (especially the verbs)? The book was burning for an unbearably long time. The intense light of the fire was smothering the natural light. I'll step through the front door of your house; I'll say that we've discovered the secret of disappearance. The twitching pages were turning into translucent moth traps. A trickle of blood dripped from the corner of my mouth, which brought a momentary relief and memories of winter. *Please, get out!* Don't say a word. I don't understand anything. You're talking to someone else. You've changed, Aleksandr. Yes. You can call me Scardanelli. A few seconds ago our bodies started changing—something was added, something else was subtracted: to deprive is to refuse. Let's write this down with the needles of our desire that stick in the corners of your eyes. From the very beginning, Heraclitus's Narcissus couldn't start his investigation of *amour*: "Who are you? Why do I love you so? Who is this haunting my memory?" Speed interrupts, is an obvious distortion— the reflection stops following its object. The elements of reflection are no longer connected.

Now I understand why. Sometimes it would rain for long periods of time. There would be mist, sun, snow, and fog, simultaneously. The snow-covered trees would burn with an ethereal whiteness against the dark violet sky. Sunglasses would immediately get covered with a layer of ice where the light granulated into bright green and orange sparks. In the morning, he rubbed his eyes with his left hand and suddenly realized, his entire being realized, that this wasn't the same hand that used to grab the thin handle of his fishing pole ("fishing pole" was the best he could do, was the only thing that came to mind to continue his zigzagging thoughts, even though it's impossible to maintain or preserve the way his thoughts felt, or tasted, and really it doesn't matter in the slightest what it was exactly that the hand was grabbing *then*); in other words, he knew, for example, how he got the scar on his middle finger.

If you close your eyes, if you unravel the threads of the day in question, it seems you can actually touch (but how?), actually re-experience the pain as your hand slipped from the crank on the well, trying as it was to stop the burning speed of the polished wood. It's even possible to feel the smell of the dust, then, to reconstruct for a moment the dark evening outlines of things in the distance. But what would remain after that moment? The imperative mood. Then he remembered too how a few months ago a new student had asked him in class what he thought about "truth." The question didn't catch him unawares; he'd actually already been thinking about it, thinking about how this word sits among other words, demanding a place between other notions and meanings that have already mastered the mechanics of their alternations.

July was coming to an end. I'm trying to narrate this story as simply as possible. Further down, it'll become clearer why I'm turning to a topic that seems incidental, not at all what I intended to focus on. There were four deaths. Three actual deaths, plus a half death. The coincidental circumstances of that day—we must restrict ourselves to speaking of the time when the decision was made—generate a disturbing story, told in fragments, making it almost impossible to assemble the pieces into something coherent, because as soon you focus on one thing, it slips away. They're writing a screenplay about it. Settings: the Anza-Borrego Desert (north of Sonora); the small town of Berkeley; College Avenue, the house of Bob Buckler, a private detective. San Quentin State Prison is an hour's drive towards

San Raphael. Cast of characters: four young men who decide one day to make a film about a car accident in the desert (what's the plot? It's unclear, except for this one particular scene) and find themselves stranded a long way from the highway.

They dump their equipment and set out for the nearest ranger station. This, I'd say, is the beginning of their film. At noon, when they begin to quarrel, one of them notices a black silhouette on top of a rolling hill they're about to pass. The person in black has a rifle in his hands. One of the men shields his eyes from the blinding sunlight and says, "I recognize that guy . . . It's Death."

What gender is death? Is it an animate noun? Or a verb? Perhaps death is a theorem that always manages in the end to prove its own accuracy on a blackboard, chalk in hand. Everyone is free to continue or end their own dialogue.

I don't know how the story goes, and I don't know how it ends. What I do know is that the young men found the idea of their car-crash film exciting, and they set the date and time for their expedition. Meanwhile, they didn't know (and neither do I) that there was another man, X, who lived in the same town. A man with a bad reputation. He was from Southern California. Two alveolar consonants weaved in the shape of a tight Indian braid. It occurred to this man to visit San Diego and the desert where he and his friends from La Jolla used to have fun.

X brings along a friend. This friend has no part in the narrative.

At the same time, Bob Buckler has two different cases on his docket—one is simple (excessive use of force in a chase; two Mexican teenagers suspected of stealing a car radio shot dead while being pursued), while the other . . . is really quite strange: a Mr. Y invites two women over for dinner, one of them his mistress of many years. After dinner, champagne, and desert, he shoots them both with a Berretta. Mr. Y is sentenced to death, and he's at San Quentin waiting for his sentence to be carried out. Naturally, Bob Buckler can't investigate both these incidents at once. He calls up Lyn Hejinian and asks her to assist him with the second case. She is to interview a wide circle of the deceased's acquaintances. On the night of her first interview, I receive a letter from her in which she shares her dark premonitions. Everyone is keeping their mouths shut. Mr. Y maintains an indifferent silence. Gradually, this case dissipates, moves to the background, while I continue to witness how our screenplay (let's call it that) unfolds.

X and his friend get to San Diego, then slowly make their way to Tijuana. They decide to visit memorial sites on the way. Their motorcycle breaks down in the desert. They leave it, along with their sleeping bags, tents, and water, take a bottle of tequila and a shotgun, and then start walking to the nearest campground. After a while, when they pass around a hill, they see a black figure on the slope with a gun in his hands. The folds of his poncho or raincoat flutter in the wind. The brims of his hat covers his face. The sun shines down, vertically.

The slow-moving dots of eagles hover over the badlands. On seeing the silhouette on the hill, X stumbles and, choking from the dust, shouts, pointing at the figure, "Hell! That's Death!" Or something like that.

He pulls out his gun and shoots at the distant figure.

The members of the film crew hear the shots, the wild cries, and run out from behind the hill. X continues shooting. Half an hour later he tries to speak to the rangers at the campground. He asks for a drink. They give him water. He asks for more. They learn that this man, high on tequila and marijuana (his friend is nowhere to be found—the plotlines are beginning to break up here) and tortured by dust and thirst, has shot down Death, pointblank, just a short ways from the camp. But the theological tinge of this incident remains rather unstable, and contrary to all expectations, fails to develop into a main theme, which can be blamed, in part, on the exhausting heat, the deaths of the unsuspecting witnesses, etc.

My dear Yelena, I'm almost done describing your lovely English dress, but before I finish, I want to ask you—and perhaps not only you: Does the delight in unity, the admiration for wholeness that the world teaches to us in our youth, really become nothing more than a grimace reflected in the smudged mirror of a razor safeguarding a delight in separation in its blade, safeguarding a blissful delirium where neither memories nor hopes are formed? I'm asking you this only to hear (one more time) how quickly the echo of my own phrase fades away—its meaning not quite clear even to me anymore.

TRANSLATION BY EVGENY PAVLOV

It's morning. There are no finches in sight, and the pecked rowan-berries underfoot are like random lines taken from any convenient poem.

The notes and correspondence of Gustave Flaubert: *On Literature, Art, and Writing*, in Russian, two volumes, purchased for next to nothing from the flea market by the Museum of Railroads, where loudspeakers mumble at you continuously from the museum's basement. It used metal-cast type. I could've haggled over the book, but it was already so (irresistibly) cheap that I just decided to "go with it."

Do you remember the days when people still used to ask each other: "What are they selling today?" You probably don't—you're still young, and anyway, what's the use of mixing beautiful fairy tales with stories from those nightmarish days. The backdrop to these memories unfolds and then darkens like the lines in a developing photograph exposed to too much light. Look at it long enough, without interruption, and you'll start seeing signs of the twilight to come. Our photograph sinks into darkness.

On a number of occasions, Ivan Alekseyevich Bunin refers to the strange, somewhat morbid impression left on him by a picture published in *Niva*, the illustrated journal; the picture had the Alps in the background, and an image of a short muscular man with a disproportionately large head. Under the picture, Bunin wrote, "There was an inscription—'*An encounter with a cretin from the mountains.*' It's hard to say how many actual cretins I've seen in my life . . ."

So, it's morning. According to all the signs, it looks like the finches had a feast here. Gertrude Stein was born on February 3rd. Snow is snow is snow, which is just an adaptation of the famous sentence from her lecture "Poetry and Grammar," which she used as an example of pure poetry—the possibility of narration without a beginning or ending.

It's either the snow or the dirt that's irritating my eyes. While I'm running my myopic finger over Stein's famous lines—"He had dreamed that he and Uncle Pierre, wearing helmets such as were depicted in his Plutarch, were leading a huge army. The army was made up of white slanting lines that filled the air like the cobwebs that float in autumn and which Dessalles called *les fils de la Vierge*"—two cretins and a singer are arguing on TV about how the English language was invented by people who didn't know how to pronounce sounds properly. They may be right.

Perhaps, too, we might be witnessing the return of a certain social need—it's difficult to say. I'm not so good at arguments and figuring out who hit whom. As an example, one of the TV people brings up an anecdote about some Englishman who couldn't pronounce the word "*pyl*'" with a soft *L* in Russian. So, instead of "dust," the stupid Englishman kept saying "heat" ("*pyl*").

Gertrude Stein once said something that was almost as famous as the sentence alluded to above (though less popular—after all, the other one was about a rose). She said: "You are all a lost generation." The consequences were astounding and well known to everyone. But let's assume that our scheduled rain got lost in the suburbs. Would this change anything? The rain got cancelled and instead, today, we have snowflakes sifting in everywhere. In order to lose something, you first need to have it. To have and have not, yet another name emerging from my memory, which doesn't change a thing in our ongoing recollections, however. This is what Clifton Fadiman said about Stein: "She was a past master in making nothing happen very slowly." Isn't memory very much like a "past master" that's good for nothing?

Aren't we compelled to remember things over and over again? Which reminds me that certain computer games don't have a "save" function, so that you can never return to a previous moment.

At this moment, however, this "past master" can easily be misread or mistaken for a "postmaster": a mediator, a dispatcher of messages. Some of these messages reach us intact, having kept their original meanings, but still—it's necessary to understand them "over again," as though they never had a past.

In the meantime, in an increasingly heated atmosphere, the advocates of correct pronunciation continue their debate, bringing concrete proofs and examples of how the language in which they communicate is, by comparison, perfect. One of these cretins is a well-known journalist. And what else should we expect from a singer?

What more can we add, my friend, after reading this: "We are entering a rather sad epoch here in France. And I, too, am becoming like the epoch."

And isn't the following remark also fascinating? "The Marquis de Sade forgot two things, cannibalism and predators, and this proves how even the greatest of people are not so great, and besides he should have ridiculed vice too, which he didn't do, and that was his mistake."

For my own part, I'll try my best to not make any mistakes.

I won't call you, I won't think of you, I won't even write about you, regardless of the enticing opening of this piece—about the morning and the finches—which got lost along the way, and which has been begging me relentlessly to continue it ever since. Any direct address creates a dangerous illusion of the validity of what's being recounted. By which I mean, imagine a person, standing alone at some crossroads or in a little town square, addressing a void: "How are you? What's going on? Would it have killed you to call?" and so on. It's hard to imagine a scenario like this if we don't acknowledge this person's absolute right to his madness: i.e., his right to establish his own routes of communication.

Now I look at my glass of beer—great, because nowadays it's possible to do so even in an opera house—and try to remember which awards some Chilean wine has won, trying (in vain) to find an appropriate if somewhat abstract plot for a future column, and simultaneously remembering a photograph of the Mechnikov Hospital where the twilight is settling on its gauze-like glass. Did you sell the car, the shells from the coast, the Eileen Fisher dress?

To tell you the truth, what I liked best was watching you look at the pecked rowanberries through the window, watching you stomp on your dress with both your feet, hearing you get in the shower and shout from there that we'd never be together again.

Direct speech presupposes the certainty that one can actually overcome the lack of expression in a given language and indeed the possibility that the original content of your speech might be meaningless. I should remember to add in a few more lines from Gertrude Stein (Why her, though? Why not, for example, Marcus Aurelius or Viktor Pelevin? Can everything be explained by the given hierarchy of the stars?): "Identity is recognition, you know who you are because you and others remember anything about yourself but essentially you are not that when you are doing anything. I am I because my little dog knows me but creatively speaking the little dog knowing that you are you and your recognizing that he knows, that is what destroys creation. That is what makes school."

Because nobody went to school, because it's still morning and there are no finches in sight, while the pecked, rotten rowanberries stick underfoot and fingers are dancing across the keyboard: "Everything is covered in frost. Do you know how beautiful you are in the morning, when the windows are covered in frost, on the day that Stein was born, when tides of grammar wash the shores of slumbering mirror-like images, and three people talk on the flickering TV screen, forced between its lines as through with a crowbar, feeling their way, unbearably slow, through the wordless tracks and outlines there, which, if we squint, become nothing more than regular patterns; these people, who, like Flaubert [let's carefully put this paragraph in scare quotes], argue about the problems of language, its use, and also about its elusive, subtle gradations of meaning, and perhaps even about love—without which it's quite impossible to write—in whose absence someone is still talking incessantly to someone else, because you have disappeared *from my side* [which I've put in italics here, despite it's being omitted in the original text], disappeared like some eloquent phrase, because this is how various conditions must be described—but turn around, and you appear in a flash, turn around again and you disappear, so there's no need to address you in so mysteriously direct a fashion."

But one shouldn't turn around. Because eventually things get dull, and with time everything will become mundane. How to get interested again. I wrote about large buildings in a different city. It seemed to me that the concept of the Tower of Babel has been completely misinterpreted by the people who are still arguing over the problems of translation. For them, the confusion of tongues exists, linguistically, as some inert spatial figure, a level field, whereas we should see it instead as an axis, with the Tower at its center—various languages spinning around it, regularly appearing and then disappearing into the darkness, inert.

I won't try to hide it: I also wrote about the horizon, which breaks out before you even get a chance to breathe in the sunrise, racing over the roofs of the big houses. Your absence, and the absence of those buildings—what this book was supposed to be about—is replaced instead with a multitude of descriptions.

I was thinking of dust particles as I was describing the stones.

. . . Then the TV offers me advice on how to raise flowers, how to get train tickets when there's a rush, and, most importantly, how to fill out my tax return painlessly.

Then begins a *vita nuova*, because, to be sure, it was morning and, soon, night.

With a feeling of synchronicity the perception of velocity begins its slow trickle into our consciousness.

TRANSLATION BY ANA LUCIC & SHUSHAN AVAGYAN

The texture of speech, rumors, and gossip is elusive, yet almost impossible to contest. It's woven thoughtlessly around us, each morning.

As a matter of fact, the number of people photographed since Daguerre's discovery exceeds the total number of people on this planet.

Some of the threads get tangled, and then, as with the ancient quipu "talking knots," memory must search the seething, ever-changing void. A photograph is not in fact an accurate means of witnessing an event, however easy it may be to accept its likeness to the original image. Witnessing presupposes documental confirmation, i.e., the affirmation (choosing and refusing) of facts that have taken place.

Today, I'm sure, I could afford, and without a feeling of remorse, the pleasure of forgetting every possible thought—each and every thought that comes at dawn, before the light, when the uselessness of birds is as exciting as the German hypothesis that "I" is not the name of a person, "here" is not a place, and "this" not a designation. Because I know for certain that thoughts are doomed to return (sooner or later). The most important thing, however, is to have some good music. "You mean, loud music?" No, I'm talking about good, slow music, the duration of which shouldn't exceed the length of a silk thread pulled through a sliver of silence.

It's not important how these thoughts of mine appear, with what cadences or in which order. Difference has no real significance. The azure hawks on the tablecloth are arranged against a purple background. It's fun to watch how spatters of mercury amalgamate.

In the late '60s, Boris Aleksandrovich Kudryakov would come to Café Saigon on Nevsky Prospect (back in those days they used to serve coffee with a glass of dry wine for people with a hangover), and sit with his gaze fixed on the grid of a misty window. Fourth table from the door, if you remember. A fact is a conventional unit for measuring the span of history. But one can't touch a fact—one can't say, "My standing here, in front of the statue of Peter, is a fact of life that can't be refuted."

But had things been the way I just described them, there wouldn't be the square, the uprising, runaway prisoners, the statue entwined with bronze vines; nor would we have the subjunctive mood and the car hood reflecting clouds drifting across the sky. Instead, we'd have falling snowflakes through the window—which would in no way suit the narrator (or me), since it would seem as though he wanted to convey the vague charm of falling snow in a letter, the envelope for which was already on the desk, but had no idea how to do it, or rather, didn't know what to do with the words presumably suitable for describing such an effect—or, in particular—the snow itself, because his ability to manipulate them (i.e., words) would be limited to his monotonous ruminations about rain (someday, after developing a passion for watching the light at sunset and wishing, as we now know, to conceal his weakness, he will say, "One must think of rain casually, in passing, as if unaware of the idea of rain—but is there such a thing as an 'idea of rain,' and, if so, what exactly would it consist of?")—here he was in his element, yet without actually seeing it; and then, despite its usual habit, the nakedness of snow revealed itself by leaving its accustomed course in the background of some window (or it may have been a wall), statue, street corner, or photographer standing in front of a group frozen in expectation of something promised by premonition, of what was already imprinted in their imagination as the idea of everything—but the difference between the "true" state of things and the things themselves, which eluded all authenticity with reprehensible ease, did not reveal itself, probably remaining in the realm of assumption, and one may consequently assume, in the realm of not-so-vivid guesses—in a disposition akin to the empty envelope lying on the desk, now a bit closer to the edge, and since it was quickly getting dark, its whiteness seemed rather abrupt in the darkened room, abrupt like the wall back then, early in that evening, which could have been mistaken for a window when seen from a particular angle, and moving away from that opening or hole in the wall, one could see the brickwork, the ivy, through which memory was seeping, bringing the person who possessed it back to the desk, the envelope, and the landscape of snow which was now finally in my full possession.

But nothing was mine. Not even the pronoun "he."

■

At home, a still life was being assembled (all on its own). This act was preceded by a lengthy preparation involving a cardboard tube and a set of lenses carefully selected from various optical devices, including a children's slide projector, all skillfully glued together. "My" relation to the "statue" was determined by a great number of prerequisites and possible consequences in whose web the action of *stand-*

ing by the statue occupies a very insignificant place. Thereafter, the most accurate temporal calculations are conducted, and the camera is hoisted on a tripod by the desk where several objects are placed in the required order: dried pomegranates, a broken pince-nez, a long-neck bottle, the skeleton of a *Corvus corax*, and a screwdriver. Maybe a roll of polished wire. A still life for the Other.

"It's all in vain, old fool." (This in Ukrainian.) "Had things been different in life, maybe I'd believe that thirty-seven is a magic number." The insignificant position of two associated objects is probably determined by both the randomness of their relationship (let us remind you that neither the "statue," nor "I" in any way "expressed" a desire to be together, to be united thus by a proposal of anticipation followed by a separation) and—if you will—one's semic insufficiency. Indeed, if the semic nucleus of the word "statue" or, say, "she" governs the layers of contextual semes, then "I" is empty (or infinite and hollow, from the very beginning). This lexeme has no nucleus whatsoever; it's nothing more than a cocoon of "contextual semes," like the knot that is a constant deflection of an illusory straight line towards its starting point.

Frankly, I'd like to say, as I did at the beginning, that "I" is reduced to a "seething, ever-changing void." But let's leave it at that.

"I" and its reflection on the threshold of "divisibility" is an opera in ink. But occasionally Levkin would visit. Wrestling with the ice on the sidewalk. A checkered book in his pocket was his counterbalance as he walked against the wind, leaning forward on the ice and sheltering under his left eyelid an amber eye that preserved its layered Mesozoic lens. His right eye was nonetheless wide open to the monotony of the embankments, to the hardy palm trees of the North, to the people who'd like to see Aleksis sneaking across the Trekhrublevy Bridge, to the balloons hovering above the Del Mar Racetrack, or to the still life ripening on Boris Aleksadrovich's desk—who sits there with his eyes fixed on the grid of a window, pulled into a whirlwind of time like muslin is drawn into a sleeper's mouth—or to the emeralds hanging as motionless in the stillness of the Russian fields as the foam in a glass of Dom Pérignon, dissolving under the moonlight.

Exposure time equaled the duration of an unhurried walk along Borovaya Street, drinking a cup of coffee, and having a random conversation. It equaled the duration of returning. The still life took four to six hours. Not counting the insomnia.

It would have been impossible to photograph yesterday's quarrel, the thoughts that followed immediately, the dream reminiscent of a daydream dreamt twenty years earlier while crossing Ertelev Street, a page from a book trapped in the algae and waterweeds of the canal, a person's face on a bus, and other things that instilled a desire to get photographed next to the statue. The scene gradually fills with hoarfrost, which slowly interlaces itself through all its indications of place and time.

Patience and one's own absence were intersecting at the point of intention.

At the time, Boris Aleksandrovich had no idea that Martha Casanave would also use a pinhole camera twenty years later to make her album *Camera Obscura* (later renamed *Mother Russia*). It was dedicated to St. Petersburg. Sooner or later the hero's voice reaches a critical point, the point of terminological branching. Of course, we'll gladly capture everything on film. Given sufficient desire and agility of imagination, one could also photograph a dream (movies work along similar principles), though each time you shot it, it would be in a different phase, a new increment, an infinitely divisible fraction of the whole.

But St. Petersburg originally belonged to the photographer Boris Kudryakov. The city offered little to this artist. But whatever it offered he shaped into remarkable forms that later appeared in an issue of *ZOOM* as photographs of what we call the "city": still lives. The editors didn't include the one I liked most, the still life of the burning book. Everything is interconnected. I'm purposely not mentioning the titles of his books. What on earth does "Cast me some soap" mean, anyway?

They once were showing his photographs in a space with white-washed walls. People approached them, looked intently, talked quietly among themselves, moving ever closer to the pictures. Some managed to walk right through those photographs. The walls were amazingly pliable. They weren't made out of mirrors. I don't know what we were made of.

Reflections open and close like a white sheet, faithless with flames.

You used to be just as you are right now; not here though—over there. If one wants to, one can reproduce, cluster by cluster, the sought-after sequence of elements. Yielding to a vertiginous kind of patience, one could extract (one by one) "every" fragment from which logic and habit would finally be able to produce the requisite texture of speech, rumors, and gossip that would then spread immediately (as though something were missing, as though an invisible error had once again crept into the impeccable equilibrium)—in order to be woven right back again. The silence of a trite metaphor is soothing. Or it would be soothing if it didn't refer to your return, which always keeps the inarticulate form of the ever-arriving future, and hits you—with the persistence of a pendulum—in unexpected places. It's different each time. Sometimes it happens when I slip and fall on the stairs. Other times your features would appear in the webs of ivy on the fence at the Botanical Garden; occasionally, a blackbird would gleam at the window (we don't have to know its name), and the scent of the sun and melting snow would vex my eyelids. Yet, other days, gasoline fumes and cigarette smoke would weave a thread of irritation; there would be an urgent desire to have a drink. But what's the point of turning around if you're already crossing the shadows cast behind you by the midday wind? I should have written: *hills*. But as far as I understand, no one intends to escape. Where would you escape to, and why? Stay where you are. Everyone is calm and in a good mood. Besides, multiple perspectives require the utmost precision of finger, eyeball, and muscle, dragging memory along the word's orbit from one layer of fog to another.

Some people fix their gazes on the grid of a misty window, others stand by a statue, and still others look through viewfinders, while a fourth kind leans over an open book at night, turning pages with a consecrated knife. Their mouths are filled with Cambrian clay, their ears—with dreams of opium.

∎

It's difficult to remember how it all started. Anyway, it happened in such a way that ever since eighth grade, those of us who couldn't leave town for the summer began gathering at Maria Sveikowskaya's house. She was a year younger than us, had moved to the city from Lvov with her parents. Her blonde ponytail, thin body, and dispassionate expression didn't stir anyone's curiosity. But she was noticeable precisely for her inconspicuousness, whose tenor constantly changed without notice, simultaneously altering and not altering her presence. She loved trigonometry and basketball more than anything else. The girls from our class preferred other kinds of sport or else were completely indifferent. She would practice with us at night; she was a first-rate player. Back then, none of us questioned why her brother went by their father's last name, Ugarov—in whose apartment we would get together a year later, feeling at-home and welcomed—while she didn't. Lieutenant General Ugarov arrived in the fall, at the beginning of the hunting season. He served in Tiksi where he was in charge of the polar aviation corps. He was there most of the time. His wife, Ksenia Leontevna, Maria's mother, a slender woman with raven-black hair and gypsy earrings, lived in Moscow, which she would leave only for her children's birthdays, because—according to Maria—"She likes it better there than the provinces (here) because she's an actress—and for other reasons too, but we need not go into them since they are irrelevant to our lives."

Meanwhile, our lives, particularly during those summers, when only three or four of us stayed in town, felt like sloppily edited home movies (even though memory diligently and indiscriminately tries to pull it all together into coherent images)—perhaps because we had a camera (their father's 8mm Convas) and filmed everything—in the streets, on the beach where we'd hang out for days on end, in the empty school to which we had the keys and where we'd develop the film every night, and then watch these "dailies" the following morning . . . Or else we'd play basketball. The gym was cool and dark because of the overgrown chestnut trees by the windows.

I'm not sure if I remember a single frame from those endless reels (whatever happened to them, anyway?), but that life comes back to me now as a collection of episodes forever lost and depressingly silent, because what appears in my field of vision are just moving mouths, faces whose expressions hint at lively conversations that are nonetheless impossible to recall. I see gestures that would have been accompanied with words like "Pour me some wine," "Where should we go tonight?" "Open the window," "Turn on some music" (a Telefunken radio), or "Pass me the cigarettes." But words have a life of their own, and I might never be able to fit them in with these pictures.

Sharp shadows on the wall. The film's low sensitivity obliges one to turn on all the lights in the room. It makes the room unbearably hot. When you turn on the light, the windows immediately blacken, and the room fills with swarms of moths and midges. A transparent black veil whirls across the walls.

Sometimes it seems I see Maria's face in close-up—her loose straw-colored hair (she's leaning over an ashtray), her collarbone, her desert-colored eyes. It seems that I can reach out and remove a crumb of tobacco from her dry, sun-burned lips, but I know (or perhaps remember?) that if I did this, I wouldn't be able to touch her shoulder, the faded strap of her dress, underneath which (as we all know very well) there is nothing—"*At night, one feels so light-headed.*"

I don't do it. I don't touch her lips. Perhaps something is distracting me . . .

I also don't do it because I don't know what's being said *there*. It would be too tedious to reinvent the conversation. But things were surely said. Sometimes phrases come back from *there*, they appear, so to speak, out of the blue—and one can't possibly know when this will happen, how they'll sound, how many of them there will be. But one doesn't have to hear them. They can be inspected.

I remember telling her (we're going up the stairs, the window on the landing is open, she sits down on the windowsill—below us, there are streets, the trembling, late-morning haze over the roofs) that each time I pronounce the word "Kiev," I see a huge, dark dumb-bell propped against the blue of the night sky.

But, she says, could your dumbbell have been a hill that you saw when first visiting Kiev as a child? Probably, I answer, that's prob-ably what it is . . . Here's another highlight: we keep planning . . . we keep saying we have to get together and "do something" because "we can't live this way any longer." To *do something* meant to go to Pechora. The Sveikowskys were directly linked to Pechora—before it was passed over to the Pototskys, Pechora belonged to them, and be-fore them, to the Zbarazhskys; the latter had acquired it from Prince Dukas who had "*bought the empty Cossack Ukraine from the Tsar of Turkey for no small sum and filled it with left-bank people to rule over them, and for his Princely Residence ordered that a famous house be built across the Bug, in Bratslawa land, in the town of Pechora.*" We didn't see the famous mansion, of course, we didn't go anywhere—no one had a driver's license—in a few days we forgot all about it, and only years later did I visit Pechora on some business trip and spend an endless humid day there in the company of a crazy tour guide and some tombstone marble.

That night we had a long, languid conversation about how there was nothing else to do in our town—"Do we really want to spend every day at the beach?" The windows were wide open. I think they opened outward, and we were lying on the floor where we had two jugs of thick Moldavian wine, a basket of apples, and a couple of ashtrays.

Then Aleksandr Kotelnikov said, "My cousin's coming from Kishinev." To which Maria's brother, who was stringing a tennis racket, replied, "She's on holiday. *That's* what you mean, right?"

The windows looked out on a steep slope covered with lindens, mulberry trees, and old fruitless plum trees. The slope went down to the river. Many years ago, this whole area belonged to Kumbare, a merchant from Odessa—and that's what it was still called, Kumbare Gardens. We used to say the beach was "kumbary."

In the mornings, I liked to watch the ferryboats pass by the granite rocks. They looked like discolored matchboxes. Across the river stretched the city: it was very different, almost flat. That's where I lived. It was impossible to separate the river from the sky.

When Maria was in eleventh grade, Lieutenant General Ugarov died in Tiksi of a heart attack. Her brother was a student in Moscow, at the Institute of Physics and Engineering. Maria visited her relatives in Warsaw a couple of times. Once it was during summer, and so I can't remember a thing from those months.

It was the fall of our last school year. Maria hadn't come back yet. Then, on a late September night when everyone in the house was asleep and I sat in the kitchen staring at the empty pages in front of me, she knocked on the window. As soon as I heard the knock, I knew that it couldn't have been anyone else at that hour. I got dressed, stepped out of the house, and we got into her father's car. It smelled of gasoline. It was a dry autumn night, and the moon hung above the trees.

High up in the heavy sky, amid the stars, I watched some bright clouds float by. "Don't tell anyone, but I was in Italy. I can get into serious trouble. You too." I didn't say anything. Then I asked her how she managed to get from Warsaw to Rome. Turning the key and looking in the rearview mirror, she said it was a complicated story and that she still needed to sort things out for herself. She also said that if I insisted and made her tell the story, we would have no time for other things. I asked about her brother. Turning onto an empty road strewn with dried leaves, she said she had no idea and asked if I wanted to run away with her. Run where?—I asked. To Italy, she said, or some other place. When I asked her what would I do there, she asked, "What are you doing here . . . ?" She drove slowly, immersed in her thoughts, while I looked out at the reflection of our car drifting in the waves of dark shopwindows. When we went upstairs to her apartment, I suddenly felt like it was the last time. Perhaps because reality had dragged its shadow off of everything. I briefly pressed my hand against the hallway wall. It was an ordinary wall. But that's what it had been all along. In the morning, as we lay there without having had a wink of sleep, she said, "It's strange, this building has six floors on one side, and nine on the other." At the end of the week, she went to live with her mother in Moscow. Thirty-four years later, I saw her at the Vantaa Airport, in Helsinki.

I was returning from Los Angeles. She was sitting with a book in her lap in a bar at the far end of the terminal where I was to board my flight to Petersburg. There was a leather bag by her feet and a glass of red wine in her hand. Next to her, a group of American students were taking pictures. She was obviously in their shot.

On the plane I asked for a beer. Much to my surprise, they brought me a free Bordeaux, though they usually charge for alcohol on "local" flights.

Let's allow ourselves one more trip: to the windowsill on that hot, myopic morning, where I see you sitting on the landing, emerging, as it were, from depths of silt, effortlessly reclining in an oval of cool echo behind whose straw-colored wing an eye-breaking space stretches out—roof tiles, streets streaming down, your dress wet to the waist. Minnows whirling around your ankles. One could add: down below (at the bottom of the page, in a footnote) stretches a field of sunflowers. As though seen from a hill. Slanting threads of dust suspended in the air:

"No one's really needed here. Never will be . . . I want to bite my hand because . . . I know it's impossible . . . still I realize how senseless it all is . . . Will I ever remember *this* . . . what do you call it . . . *happiness*? Give me a cigarette." A lens in a bundle of slippery, yellow grass.

But don't lose sight of this: there, beyond the crossing, further down, in the bluish haze of burning peat bogs, is the brickyard. Who's talking? The power lines.

■

Marseilles. May, Saturday, 2:20 P.M. A bar across from Garibaldi Hotel.

—For your information, I changed the word order in "a crazy tour guide and some tombstone marble," she says. Instead, I have "in the company of a tombstone tour guide and some crazy marble." And this rearrangement made me think about displacement. Let's say we write: "At point B arrives the train and point A from departs." When human consciousness is unable to *make sense*, i.e., to *perceive* something, it rearranges everything, "restores" the sentence that was written, as it were, out of order, and puts everything in its "normal" (A to B) order.

So, the reader doesn't *see* the sentence that you're "actually" writing, your sentence is immediately "explicated," i.e., put in the right order ("The train departs from point A and arrives at point B") the moment the eye *captures* the text. One remembers people who suffer from a relatively well-known affliction that has them read the word "dog" as "cat." However, it seems to me that the paragraph starting with "That night we had a long, languid conversation," which later mentions the Institute of Physics and Engineering, and then the paragraph about the visiting cousin (what were you intending to do with her?), and then, again, the car ride, are all the beginnings or middles of other stories that have nothing to do with this one.

But please, don't edit out the General and the "Kumbare." Imagine how wonderful it would be if a certain M left for Moscow immediately after her father's death and then reappeared, thirty-four years later, in the same sentence, but another airport. By the way, how does a German statement sound in German?

—*Ob meine die Bücher sind? Ob mein das Bein ist? Ob meine die Sprache ist?* But this probably isn't what you meant.

■

I could have said that oblivion crystallizes history as it rids the latter of the excessive moisture of "reality" (for "reality," see "imagination"—

footnote not included here). But until the time is right, it's not appropriate to say anything about oblivion that's more or less comprehensible. Similarly, a child doesn't know the word "immortality" ("The Serpent of Time swallows their forms . . ."—*The Amduat*). "Immortality" reveals itself much later—eternally unchanging—in the form of thoughts, as we mentioned at the beginning, which come and go, only to reinvent their correlation with one another. And in order not to succumb to the charms of permanence, they often transform themselves into various shapes that aren't always approved of by society or its governing bodies. However, what's more interesting is the colorblindness of intention that intersects patience with one's own absence (transparence). The act can't expose one's purpose: "I had no other choice."

An unsent letter written twenty-three years ago:

> [. . .] cold spring sunsets over the islands. The inscrutable light moves along the wallpaper and the spines of books. The pale blue sky reflected on the wall almost reaches my temples and the tree branches outside the window, or rather, their crowns. I'm addicted to studying the light lying around me. At first, it merely fascinates me, then—it turns into an obsession. Light that subsides with time, rejecting the existence of the things it once embraced. Would a description change if things changed their positions on a map? What if we were violent towards them? For example, what if we switched adjectives, i.e., attributes?
>
> One day I decided to give up alcohol—the swiftness of the colors around me, fringed with phosphorescent light-

ing, and the abrupt temporal transitions that used to amuse me so much were starting to lose their charm, turning into—not difficult to guess—irritating oxymorons preventing me from enjoying the sunset, watching it as it burned my book spines, enjoying the people by the statue, the photographer with his camera by his eyes, the parked car around the corner with its raven-black hood reflecting a woman fixing her stocking . . . I quit alcohol with the same indifference I gave up marijuana, literature, and the house where I grew up, when I was young. Which gave me (for an unthinkably brief moment, however) the rarest pleasure, unfathomable clarity—stunning, polar bareness, and a sense of complete negligence regarding my own life—a feeling that you made me experience for the first time, and which, however, fills me with uncertainty . . .

■

Last summer, walking with his mother, a boy from one of the ninth-floor apartments saw a pigeon trapped between the panes of a nearby window. He tore his hand from his mother's, dashed to the fluttering bird, and dissolved with the pigeon behind the window. The window remained. The frame is never included in the price of a painting. One always ends up paying more.

The birds will lead children and clowns beyond the Horn of Sunset, into the valleys of Duat. Incidentally, Charles Olson wrote at some length about one of these birds. Why kingfishers and not pterodactyls? It's not that manners, customs, and habits are impediments, or that they, more than anything else (and I insist on this non-correspondence), move some people to study ornithology.

In another place, yet also *here*, another son blinded his mother so that she wouldn't see him killing her. Obviously, as one should expect, he didn't find any money. That's what always happens. The birds must be laughing at us . . . I wonder if they remember . . . what? Say, for example . . . happiness? And if they do laugh at us—when . . . ? In spring? At noon? At the edge of the forest? Was the extinction of certain civilizations a matter of their evolutionary helplessness, their impotence? I'm inclined to speak up and remind them: they never used to talk about inflation, children, Jews, and trips to America so much.

Last November, in Moscow, when Boris Aleksadrovich Kudryakov was receiving the Turgenev Prize for his contribution to the development of Russian prose, he leaned over my shoulder and whispered in my ear: "If they knew that it was a book by Turgenev that I set on fire in that photograph you like so much, I wouldn't be getting this prize."

By now it should be clear what was used in the making of my favorite still life: a) 2 bottles of Rkatsiteli wine—consumed with Boris Smelov; b) 1.5 liters of kerosene; c) 2 boxes of matches. The photograph was taken in the shadow of a railway embankment near Gorelovo Station.

"And in the meantime"—like the black crystal in the mouth of a mole, or a fish between silver blades, demanding to be released from your fingers. Is the photograph taken by the statue documented evidence? If so, of what?

One could suggest that the desire to take photographs lies elsewhere than in producing documents. We do not take photographs in order to *preserve* something, to *not forget* (i.e., lose) someone, nor even to add to the world's archive yet another image of something, the meaning of which evaporates immediately the moment it's been touched by vision. It's more likely that we take pictures in order to come closer, yet again, to an unsolved contradiction: the desire to "photograph" something lying beyond the jurisdiction of the eye—and likewise beyond light, shadow, chemistry, polygraphs, time, memory, hope, etc.; something that preceded by a vague certainty that this "future" image (not yet extant) has already been thought, already been in the mind, yet without a concrete "image"; the act of manipulating physical substances (such as glass, plastic, metals), distributed in time and shaped by the logic required for the execution of an "intention," is in fact a method of "visually" demonstrating this "mental figure," which itself asserts the reality of one's own existence whenever it becomes necessary to make such an affirmation, or else *repeat* it—which affirmation and/or repetition are, perhaps, ideal, tautological rituals that don't derive *something* from *something else* but merely change one's perspective. When "experiencing" or "studying" a photograph, however, one is, in fact, less inclined to start an investigation, to engage in an aesthetical *einfühlung*, into the simultaneity of absence/presence.

What we want, simply, is to study *ourselves* through photographs, ourselves looking out onto the field of depiction; and our desire to conclusively combine the outside view with the inside is like bridging "tomorrow" with "yesterday," deleting the space "in between," which is of course impossible, since we can exist only in this "between." In our desire to overlap these concepts—we are caught "between." The present will never be "complete." The figure of death doesn't clarify a thing, no matter how many times it's exposed. One hardly ever succeeds in even grasping a simple feeling of empathy.

Every photographic attempt to capture a wedding, vacation, funeral, statue, roof, bed, etc., etc., etc., is yet another meaningless attempt to convince ourselves that we exist. Unfortunately, we are never wholly convinced. Not even when we're slitting our wrists, or finding out that we've inherited an apartment in SoHo. What follows instead are bad weather forecasts, or pages of writing, or worst of all—a line from a translation, distorted beyond recognition.

The original gets lost for reasons that are entirely unclear. But first, as a rule, the language in which it was written must disappear. Everything becomes confusing.

After how many editorial changes, corrections, and alterations, all determined by the aspiration to reinvent a text (and stay faithful to the source, perhaps even to truth?) should we consider a certain version as *canonical*, a good substitute for the original? We might as well ask whether one can *own* a book or a language. And yet, sometimes, ordinary passersby entice the birds to give them an answer. Ordinary people. Not necessarily military officers. Not even people with cameras. People like you and me. They like using the Internet. They enjoy Heraclites. Beer. Feasts. Auspices. People who know about organic chemistry. *Les connoisseurs.*

This third option is given as a pre(con)text: the possibility of yet another landscape substitution.

This is why the imagination so easily paints another picture—according to Boris Ostanin at whose summerhouse Boris Aleksandrovich was a frequent guest. We see his figure slowly disappearing into the deserted steppe. He's carrying on his shoulder a pinewood desk that he built with his own hands. It's held together with aluminum wire in places, the kind of wire that reminds me of the pince-nez on the desk in front of the cardboard lens, taped together with blue tape (we haven't forgotten the screwdriver, wire, or brickyard). It used to be called aircraft tape (blue sky, speed, foreign countries) and was almost impossible to get. The place, where I've finally found myself, is as simple as a child's board game. Everything in it echoes everything else. Coincidences aren't always believable. And they don't always count. Obliqueness has its own charm.

Which is why, sooner or later, the passerby knocking at the door is given a warm welcome, and after a short period of time (overcoming embarrassment, he had just begun talking about the friends of his youth, his first love, his secret dreams and student years) he awkwardly discovers that he's back knocking on that same door again. But is it the same door? Is it the same passerby? Same telephone number? Same photograph? Same Jerusalem? One thing is clear: in half an hour, we catch ourselves spying on a man sitting at his desk (in a space exposed to the wind and drizzling rain) and bearing some small resemblance to what we've been calling "we." Though the man isn't concerned with anything. He's writing.

"*They've all gone their separate ways. The sandman meditates: I came into this life like I was going to work. And what do I get for it?*" There aren't many choices.

The man forces out word after word.

The letters run in the rain and pour into the message. The man, no doubt, is reading the message as he inscribes his letters.

In the message, unflinching, unfolding via ink blots, there are detailed instructions on how to correlate one letter with another, one word with another, and then the rest with rain, paper, war, objects, fear, the hexagram of "fragments," toothaches, questions, history, tobacco smoke, poetry, foolishness, you name it . . .

The message also suggests that neither he nor you will receive a thing for it—this work is done *gratis*.

TRANSLATION BY EVGENY PAVLOV

Snapshots turn the eye into a curious animal.

In its own eyes, Petersburg arises effortlessly as a collection of postcards, unstable reflections of rumors about its eventual fate.

It's as simple as playing with toy soldiers—little figurines scattered around, the smoke of puppet battles, history on a tiny scale, the nonexistence of death, the clinking of glasses; yet the conversation is taken beyond the cover, beyond the field of conventions. Still, the landscape remains unchanged.

The table of contents is worn to holes. Through them one sometimes happens to catch a glimpse of the sun, during the white nights. For me, this is probably the third June I've seen with snow on the trees. If we could sell *this* light, we would live like Kuwaitis—until the ruin of Hollywood. In July the heat of blasting music fades, candlelight gets dim, exotic trophies get covered with a patina of chance, and the mirage of yet another golden season rises up behind your back.

But the gold doesn't stick. Someone is holding a glass or a phone receiver, someone else has a perfect knowledge of geographical maps or at least playing cards; many circumstances turn out to be much more complicated than they appeared in spring, or simply last year. Only mathematics seems transparent; everything else seeks a superior position, or else to be exiled in history.

■

The swallows are back under the roofs, and the sparrow orgies at five in the morning have stopped.

The advantage of postcards or news briefs, it seems, is that they give us only one snapshot at first, then another one, and later a few more. In this context, "the journalist" is like a character from a folk-tale, trying to assemble a name from fragments of frozen water, only the last letter always slips away like a melting crystal.

But no matter how many postcards attempt to reconstruct this city from various redeemable angles, the real map always appears on the table, inexplicably connecting the sites of an unfinished mo-torway, Taurida—long without water, the sleepless gulf, pedestrians caught in a certain aperture of the slanting muslin of movement, dew on ghostly tram tracks, myopic opera-house boxes . . . An endless debate—is *this* the city?

What we have listed here is enough for the Great Wall of China. The dissensions are also included in the sum of property and dis-tance, along with world festivals, fountains, phantasms, or discus-sions on how to turn the city into another cosmopolitan Havana—although its harbor has been and will be there till the end of time.

∎

One can distinguish various contours in the optics of Petersburg. To some, they appear as harmonious colonnades of reason and splendor amid curtains of nostalgia. To others—as intricate configu-rations of power and its attributes. And yet to a third group, these outlines form the impenetrable concerns of everyday life, where fragile things, half-abraded by repetition, surface in unexpected arrangements, revealing a remarkable uniqueness, like, for example, a newspaper photograph hidden behind some wallpaper, a brass thimble lost somewhere on the floor, Arsenyev's third volume (published by GosLit), laughter behind the wall—and if jasmine blooms are in season, nobody will notice the burning garbage cans around the corner.

I don't remember all the details, but it seems that in the '60s a man was filmed sleeping in New York (for twelve hours?). The man slept, the camera kept filming. Reel after reel, a sleeping man: though they didn't capture his dreams, these were left on the cutting-room floor. Sokurov filmed the Hermitage much later. May we assume that the sleeping man dreamed he was sleeping, and that the camera was relentlessly documenting—in phases—his trembling half-existence, and the running shadows of the receding day or approaching sunrise?

.

Can we presume that Petersburg dreams too: dreams of how it emerges from the endlessly self-erasing descriptions of its own, old self?

But splitting is always a parting from the whole. And sooner or later something other than a harrowing disappointment or disconnection is formed from this irreducible parting. At the same time, this bifurcation, this parting results not from the intention to merely look at yourself, but to look at yourself looking "at yourself" with enchantment. In some sense Petersburg literature owes a great deal to such an enterprise, and thus its best descriptions can never be brought full circle.

■

At times, one might come across extremely minimal spaces, visually speaking, just past those descriptions, such as the unsophisticated five-story Khruschevka buildings, junked cars on the pavement and lovely wastelands drowning in amethyst blooming-sally, broken bricks and outbreaks of coltsfoot bushes.

Here, the same postcards reveal something completely different. Imagine the number of edits they'll have to undergo. Sometimes the black peat burns beyond the horizon of Porokhovye. The air thickens. Time becomes tangibly reified, and *fact*, *message*, *event* enter the field of dangerous proximity.

And yet, the thickness of the air—like silence or a ringing in the ear—can hardly ever be listed as an event.

■

A "snapshot" of a city, as such, probably doesn't exist at all. The association with another city, country, language, memories of books read or lost in Cairo, Paris, Stockholm stretch the transparent layers of the fabric that we'd like to (erroneously) consider as "the only" impression and final conclusion.

I'm not fully convinced that I've listed everything in the correct order. Things may appear differently. Likewise, a certain event can be made into a fact. There is, doubtlessly, a message in between. Does it change anything? It's hard to tell. First of all, it probably changes the person who creates it. Then the message transforms into something else, another element is added. Sometimes it may turn into dreams, sometimes into a self-sufficient fact.

After a while, you frantically dial a number and tell the person on the other end that the panorama isn't composed of a mosaic of snapshots arranged along the axes of values and valuables, and that it's not a matter of taking a few steps back so as to see everything as a whole, but that actually there's no such space as "back," just as there are no final facts full of the promise of actually experiencing an event.

■

I don't like snapshots, they kill the imagination, turn boredom into a sentimental hedonism, and consequently, to irony. It would be quite right to say that Petersburg became a collection of postcards a long time ago: voluptuous harpists leaning lasciviously at the foot of Titian's bed in the light of the flaming Rostral Columns, or the lamps of a nightclub whose entrance is crowded with yet another folio of more-than-familiar faces, a couple of which haven't been above appearing on gaudy book covers, and others, to whom one can grant a thoughtless nod, appearing in newspaper headlines.

A familiar sign or billboard might flash somewhere—*fassbinder, beer, chekhov, a message to man* . . . Signs can also be a Primer, and a quite bizarre one at that: they can help one unlearn how to read by reducing one's consciousness to a world of arrows and symbols.

It's odd that no one publishes photo albums (with morocco bindings) of train station kiosks and carefree people on lawns, images of Grazhdanka, Porokhovye, Vesely Poselok, and other bleak suburbs . . . Could it be that these spaces are substantially less valuable than the Hermitage and its surroundings?

Frankly, I like spaces that happen to be on the "brink." I come from a place like that, and I've gotten more out of life than anyone could possibly imagine. But the snapshot we're after shouldn't be made up of multiple, competing postcards juxtaposed with one another. Nor should it consist of cross-stitches between obligation and inevitability.

Rather, it should consist of facts rooted in experience based on events inspired by dreams (it's simply impossible that no camera has captured them yet); and after that we should have, again, a description, a retelling, a rumor, and yet another encounter with some event.

In its thoughtless speech—this is where Petersburg's notorious mythology seems to originate. Its love of shells, the precipitance of its barreled river, and its carefully concealed passion for duality and mirrors. But you notice a shadow on the asphalt, the rustling of a sick poplar, a dirty fourth-floor window—love probably never passed through here—and high up, the swift swallows, sowing canvasses of continuity. In response, you make a gesture filled with uncertainty.

∎

Was it there or here that memories, stubbornly evading public attention, were really written and sent off into the future—amazing memories, in their beauty and restraint? Was it there or here that subtle ideas were proclaimed, construing unnoticeably revolutionary manifestos that were supposed to change the world?

But those ideas couldn't change the geography, or even our methods of adapting it. The weather hasn't been the same for years.

Permanence is one of the facets of metamorphosis. I agree, to a certain degree, that we *do indeed* consist of total fabric of the same "memories" that ceaselessly transform us into *something else*. Sometimes, with a bit of a stretch, we can liken "memories" to roads. Some are broken, while others consume dreams, bicycle wheels, time, money, and anticipated turns.

■

Petersburg, they say, is somewhat different from other cities. Indeed, many cities were "created" by means of seeds and residue and then slowly bloomed with noble nodules, falling into an endless lethargy of efficiency. Let's imagine how hundreds and thousands of histories unfold. And we, looking out as though from the back window of a car, see things, objects that appear as if from nowhere, inscribing themselves in the field of vision of our present time.

Then everything—everything the landscape consists of—"ages," as it were, shrinks, and disappears beyond the horizon. And everything becomes, on the one hand, memory, and on the other hand—in the past (it's unclear what comes first and what second)—a residue of vision, a residue that we know still exists. Let's use a familiar figure of speech: time passes, its residue remains.

Sometimes cities symbolize that residue. Petersburg, however, is not the residue of history. It's a place created by a momentary force, a momentous and destructive lightning bolt that struck and reversed our vision. This is where the difference lies, and hence creates a different perspective—even if the perspective comes from a juxtaposition of postcards, from where this city will only begin to exist, creating a certain anticipation in an outsider. And it will never be defined or trespassed because it exists *within its own limits.*

This may be why, for many, it becomes a place for the work of idleness and exclusion, exclusion to the margins of understanding, where Petersburg appears first and foremost as a *pure form of desire.*

TRANSLATION BY EVGENY PAVLOV

For the traveler there inevitably comes a moment when his or her memories are converted into small change. This kind of money has the habit of disappearing with a clang as it settles darkly at the bottom of various fountains or in a variety of receptacles along passageways. Passageways are dimly lit, umbrellas sometimes lie in a pile, "just in case." On occasion there's even a faint odor of basil in the air.

Memories settle at the bottom of words, turning what's seen in daylight into stranger-than-strange figures and into never-before-seen images. The dream spectator, the contemplator of the fleeting laws of impalpable universes, is easily recognizable on the streets—whether in Marseille, Petersburg, or New York. Their faces are lit by the flames of still unextinguished visions, their arms mechanically groping among the shadows for something to lean on. Sitting on the stoop of a brownstone at Park Place in Brooklyn, I began to have the foretaste of a mysterious paragraph from an as-yet-unwritten letter to my friend Valery Savchuk: "Like a millstone, the merging of space and dislocation of time grinds down previous experience—an experience that seemed unshakeable, had the self-assurance of allegory; it gave rise to a string of explanations that immediately freed time of all its obligations in arcades of metaphor which were bestowed in multitudes to the imagination." In truth all I was trying to do was remember the ineffably warm nights in the Old Port of Marseille.

I don't want to forget the plane trees—in spite of the fact that at present I'm finding it very difficult to apportion them among the cities. And perhaps it's not even necessary: at the back of the Community Bookstore on 7th Avenue, behind the books, I've happily discovered a small café.

Books, in any quantity, can be taken down from the shelves and brought into the café, to be read to your heart's content. They can even be taken out into a small garden, where an ash tree out of Turgenev is wrapped around a plane tree. Without a care in the world and with a cup of coffee, you can now set to work as if in a library. Of course it's cooler out in the garden.

On one of the tables I find some pages left behind by someone. They contain a rather dry account of the history of the so-called Voynich manuscript—a manuscript of mysterious provenance, written in an indecipherable language or code that cryptologists of the time of its discovery were unable to break. In 1961 the manuscript was bought by the New York book dealer G. P. Krauss for twenty-four thousand dollars. Later, its value was assessed at one hundred and sixty thousand dollars, but after a long and unsuccessful search for a buyer Krauss donated it to Yale University. The first known mention of the manuscript dates from 1666, from the hand of Johannes Marcus Marci, in a letter in which he explains that it was obtained by the Bohemian Prince Rudolf II for six hundred ducats, then an enormous sum.

Like the last time, the sight of New York, as one flies down into it, recalls nothing so much as a scullery of cockle shells at the bottom of an ancient galleon. The only difference is that it's not quite so deeply submerged, up in the clouds. As soon as you get used to hearing several languages spoken at once, the surroundings suddenly lose their fifth dimension and the world returns to the realm of normal things, such as the heel of my shoe, ground down from too much walking, the reflection of the setting sun cast with seeming indifference by a passing subway train on the Manhattan Bridge, the ring of a telephone, a receipt from a liquor store, or a tearful meeting with Avital Ronell in a labyrinth of offices at NYU.

As was the case five years ago, Chilean wine is readily available. Although Los Vascos is generally considered the best, I personally prefer the '98 Las Casas. Tower Records—that bottomless pit of music and whispers in which, in what now feels like an incredibly distant spring, Sergei Kuryokhin whiled away his sleepless hours— still stands at the corner of Broadway and Great Jones Street. NYU's School of Arts and Sciences has moved and is now located only a few steps from here. By the way, it takes six years of study to be certified to prepare Japanese sashimi. It's doubtful that they teach it at the university in spite of the fact that they call it a school of arts, and that on the floor below me I can see doctors in white coats. But the Japanese are tolerant. They even tolerate their status as a minority. In brief, they are able to deal with the "eternity" of the Big Apple without sacrificing the ability to express their obvious feeling of personal dignity. It's possible that this is not unique to the Japanese, and in part this is perhaps why I've never seen a single ad for chewing gum here, not even on television. One must assume that this is because no one chews it. But they do drink coffee! In fact, it's fairly good and decently served. Starbucks, the nationwide chain of American cafés, is clearly not doing particularly well downtown. A McDonald's-style café is still a McDonald's; but Italian cafés are everywhere in SoHo, and their prices are through the roof. One thing is certain: given the incredible pace of life here, there's no truth to our fairy-tale New

York café with a single wobbly table and calico curtains. Nevertheless, one curtain did beckon to me from a pile of Chinese jade eggs and Soviet badges that were being sold at a local flea market: a faded reproduction of Edward Hopper's *Early Sunday Morning*.

The speed—or rather the slowness—with which the painting returned to its place in my head was discouraging, and it was only on Sunday, in New Jersey, that I saw something that the artist had kept silent about: I saw the fine line that separates emptiness from plenitude. I recalled, like the memory of something that never happened, and which sinks then to the cunning bottom of words, to the bottom of the bottle, something that glimmers in Chekhov but that in Boris Akunin's sequel to *The Seagull* pales with startling rapidity.

In New Jersey it's someone by the name of Fandorin who seems to play the role of trivial ornament, something like that strip of Columbus Avenue with painted doorways and windows that don't always coincide exactly with the real ones. The prices here suit everyone's budget. This includes even Vladimir Kanevsky, who has managed to dig himself a real sculptor's lair on the second floor. He bears this hell (ninety degrees Fahrenheit plus another one thousand degrees when he fires up his kiln) with the equanimity of a Roman legionnaire staring straight into an air conditioner. Or vice versa. The important thing, he says, is that you can see the stars and there's a good bakery downstairs. He doesn't care when the electricity comes on or how the movers handle his sculptures that have just returned from a European show. And what's the use anyway, when, in addition to everything else, "Indian summer" has descended? Everybody's on roller skates and nobody sleeps. It's a pity that Whitman never wrote any odes to garbage trucks. I think he could have started one off like this: "I celebrate and sing you, giant American garbage trucks / Devouring our past each morning / And with the ease of a serrated knife / Carrying off all traces of predawn dreams."

Happily, at the corner of Barrow and Mercer streets (I'm leaving now, have already left, it's Wednesday here), there's a piano bar called J. C. Winston's. On top of the piano there's a sign: Don't touch the piano, don't put your glass on the piano, and no shooting. Inside, on the door, there's another: Respect Your Neighborhood.

This is probably just in case someone's got the keys of power in his or her pocket.

CAST ME SOME SOAP

One of those unnoticed phenomena, or rather one of those phenomena that has imperceptibly become part of daily life, thanks to the Internet, and just as imperceptibly changed daily life itself, is electronic mail. However, those limp but tirelessly persistent lamentations by the defenders of the pen and the admirers of Gutenberg—for some reason this reminds me of a recent summer conference, not of birds but of writers, in Moscow—about how we are precipitously abandoning our beloved galaxy, about how the good old days of the ruled page, neurasthenic rough drafts, and postal horses are becoming part of the past, about how we are surrendering to the world of the visual image, have proven to be little more than a primitive framework to describe a rather different, independent course of events.

The picture that can occasionally be glimpsed in this design is a monotonous one, and full of a facile melancholy. On one side are the scribes, masters of an impeccable "rondo," equipped with candles, ink, night-thoughts, and the date "Martober 2034"; in a word, everything that mourns for a kind of poetry that's disappearing before our eyes. On the other side a group of perfidious, virtual monsters wearing black leather gloves and helmets who take the stage armed with terrifying jargon, whose lexicon is incomprehensible but whose clear intention is to destroy "what we cherish."

In reality, the logic of these changing textures and modes of writing bear witness to something altogether different, and applies to their various manifestations. Generally speaking, each new mode seems richer than the preceding one; and while the new one does indeed repress what came before it, it also adds new possibilities to what already exists. Silent films were replaced by talkies. Then came color. And then a new format. Then nonstop television, on which those old, silent, black-and-white movies sometimes provide an unexpected bit of pure pleasure. However, the means by which new forms of writing subsequently influence "writers" is a history of a different kind.

In the course of the last ten or so years, with the creation of the Internet and the Web, we have seen not only a gradual revolution in the perception of time and space, and consequently of the possibilities of expression, but also—strange as it may seem—one other fundamental phenomenon: a return to writing, perhaps to virtual writing, but nevertheless to writing. It turns out that we have unconsciously come full circle, returning to "paper" in spite of all the ardent speeches in defense of the new, digital order of things. Indeed the Internet has turned us back toward the past because, as Adam Gopnik has written, the Internet is a kind of writing, given that it is literally *written* "from beginning to end."

This can of course be refuted: even assuming that you're right, what is the "carrier," then, of *this writing*? Can it still be considered "writing"? Paper can be touched. A book is a tangible, physical object; moreover, it has a smell: printers' ink, manufacturing chemicals, etc. And how priceless is writing paper itself, its special, unique odor and color, to which literature has paid much homage so often! Finally, what separates the first, primordial sign etched in stone from the image on a computer screen? To this imaginary question I give the following answer: what is most important to consider are the changes in the concept of materiality, as well in the system of concepts—a process stretching back over the last hundred years—relating to the very possibility of describing any material object whatsoever. This object, the description of which previously relied on the coordination of the concepts "beginning and end" (every object had both), is now conceived as some kind of oscillating point of a perpetual "now," a definitive account of which is extremely difficult, if not impossible, to obtain. Indeed, isn't it rather naïve to claim that we can feel a sign, as if it were a slab of painted, reinforced concrete that could be dragged up to the forty-fourth floor?

All in all, "to be online" signifies, on the one hand, a perpetual "now," real time, but on the other hand it means reading words written by others, no less than typing out one's own words, addressed to someone else. Even game sites can't function without words. (Not to mention pornography sites, with all their pockmarked explanations and dubious stories.) As for electronic mail itself, there's no way to deny its textual character—of course, with the addition of instantaneous transmission. But only this transmission, nothing more.

Even five years ago most of us relied on the telephone for contact, with perhaps a dozen or so letters written per year. This is not to say that there were no exceptions to this rule, no champions of epistolary prose; but the reasons for their passion were of a different order than ours. In their enterprise, the border between personal journal and the outside world was, so to speak, effaced from the start, where the functions of interlocutor were transferred not to the "I" itself, nor to an imaginary future reader, but to an extant recipient whose role was akin to that of a publisher.

Neither a telephone nor videophone offers the possibilities of e-mail, for this simple reason: *writing.* Written language has the inherent ability to create a salutary barrier, a kind of second skin or distance that allows one to disappear from sight whenever one wants. This is a space in which no one can deprive you of the right to instantaneous solitude on this otherwise all too overcrowded, unlivable island.

NYU Professor Marek Skalsky has his office directly across the hall from mine. As far as I know he is the only person within a radius of fifty kilometers who, with unfeigned and malicious glee, beats on the keys of an altogether unelectric typewriter in what can only be called a holy intoxication. It's certainly within the realm of possibility that his performance on the typewriter is itself some mysterious part of his life's work. This perhaps explains why so many of his colleagues, from various departments, sneak up to his door and, with an expression of mystical horror mixed perhaps with ecstasy, listen hypnotized to the banging of the keys, as if to a heavenly choir.

In order to connect with Professor Skalsky you've got to catch him in the hall or elevator. Knocking on his door is useless, for the obvious reason. His fax machine broke down sometime back in the twentieth century. The sound of the telephone sends him into spasms of rage because the first words he always hears have something to do with questions about his e-mail address.

I drop in to see Eliot, a professor in the Slavic Department and a specialist on the mystery writer Alexandra Marinina, then return to my desk to write this last line: If I'm not right, then cast me some soap.

IN THE COUNTRY

Considering the quiet of the morning and the placid expressions on the faces of the passersby, you might take this world-famous neighborhood for a country village on a fine, cloudless morning. But this impression would be deceptive.

At eight thirty in the morning the neighborhood is already aboil with activity, like hydrogen peroxide bubbling on a cut. Suddenly and irrevocably. The Dutch bought Manhattan from the Indians in 1626. At that time the island was covered with forest, and elk and moose rambled freely—in a word, nature successfully played its role of a stern but beautiful mother until it was conquered by a tobacco plantation.

By eight you already have to elbow your way inside Café-Café on Green Street. The rustle of papers, a crepe de chine crackling of notebook computers, cell phones trilling softly—a cup of iced coffee in hand. The ice gives sharpness to outlines. I'm waiting here to meet with the documentary filmmaker Jackie Ochs, who has lived in SoHo her whole life. Recently the Museum of Modern Art opened a Downtown location: Jackie's apartment building shares its entryway with the new museum. "It's gotten safer and cleaner." That's no surprise. Peter Aleshkovsky, for example, was born in the Tretiakovsky Gallery.

Both Jackie's apartment and the museum are located on lower Broadway, a few doors down from Houston Street. It's a stone's throw from my office to Green Street. In 1731 the English Naval Commander Sir Peter Warren bought part of a plantation and, the chronicles tell us, built a marvelous estate for himself. He called the area Greenwich. Jackie is supposed to have arranged a meeting with Betsy Sussler, the publisher of *Bomb* magazine.

In 1983 *Bomb* devoted several of its pages to material about the culture of St. Petersburg. In those days the magazine was still large format. The cover photograph shows Boris Smelov standing by a gloomy-looking Yekaterininsky Canal. SoHo, in fact, is not technically part of Greenwich Village, which ends at Canal Street: indeed, the word "SoHo" simply means South of Houston. Everything north of it is "NoHo."

At the end of the nineteenth century the entire neighborhood was rebuilt—indeed, it was here that the practice of raising "poured concrete facades" was first used. Initially, its purpose was merely to reinforce the already-standing wood and brick structures with a mixture of "Greek Revival," "Palazzo," and other styles. By the 1920s the population of the area radically changed: flouting bourgeois values, the residents of Greenwich Village became famous for their "free" lifestyle. In 1970, a powerful lobby of artists managed to have a city law put in place that granted loft-space to anyone who could prove that he or she was an artist. These lofts are protected by rent control, which means that rents can't be raised as long as a given inhabitant continues to reside there. This literally compulsory attachment to SoHo was in part responsible for the difficulties encountered by the next generation of artists to find somewhere to live in the city—in the 1980s they were forced to settle in the East Village. Such are the dynamics of this bit of micro-geography.

It's a five-minute walk to the offices of *Bomb*. Unfortunately, Betsy Sussler isn't there. We subsequently learn that she thought the meeting was to take place on another day. And that the person she was expecting to meet with was someone altogether different than me. Editors are the same everywhere.

"Timing. It's always a matter of timing," says Jan Kroeze, Jackie's husband and head of JKLD Incorporated. "And time constantly changes direction."

Formerly a lighting director in various theaters, Jan turned to the world of *haute couture* in the late '80s and is currently one of its foremost figures. He tells me that lighting for the theater and for fashion are two totally different activities: "In the theater light is used to bring out a particular shade of meaning, to create the most appropriate context for the director's idea or to help with a performance. In the fashion world, light is used either to make a woman look as attractive as possible or to create a desired atmosphere on the runway—romantic or urban, soft or harsh, and so on. But of course the most important thing is to make the woman look beautiful. Are the top models actually beautiful in real life? . . . well, yes—how shall I put it? They're normal, nice-looking girls. After a weeklong fashion show we usually celebrate with a party . . . there's smoking, drinking, dancing, and the like. The girls look horrible, exhausted, totally worn out. That's when I go to work: I make the light soft, tender, delicate."

On the apartment's balcony Jan tells me about his incredibly tight schedule. Victoria's Secret has added a spring show for Cannes to run parallel to the film festival. This means he'll need ten fully-equipped trailers from Europe in addition to the three trailers of computer equipment that will be shipped from America; and it all has to be ready in a week. Generally the season starts in June—in Paris and Milan. In July they go to New York. Then September in New York again.

Jan tells me that his first payment for work as a lighting director was in the form of a suit. The suit cost twenty-eight thousand dollars.

"No," I hear Jackie say. "It's not worth waiting. Let's go to her place."

She means to Betsy Sussler's. But it turns out that Jackie herself can't go. I go alone. Everything's close by. One more iced coffee "to go." At her office they tell me that she's on her way to the office; or rather that she called from the subway to say that she was on her way.

The first issue of *Bomb* was published in 1981. The aim of the magazine was fairly simple: to allow artists to give their opinions about what they think about art, not only in New York but worldwide. Or more exactly: to create a forum for the discussion of the question of what makes art art. The main thing was to allow artists, critics, poets, writers, directors, and musicians to speak directly to one another—the "interviewer" was taken out of the loop because the magazine's interest was in "the deeply personal" way that these questions were posed in the artist's own work.

By calling it *Bomb* the editors were acting on the presumption that they would only produce a few issues—but the explosion lingered and the magazine still exists nineteen years later. In 1999, Gordon and Breach released three volumes of the best interviews: *Speak Art!*, *Speak Theater and Film!*, *Speak Fiction and Poetry!*. The press run of each issue is twenty-eight thousand and *Bomb* is read by approximately one hundred-twenty thousand people. Advertisements and fairly serious material are published side by side. Imagining NLO with color advertisements for Absolut vodka and Italian shoes, I came to the conclusion that there would be nothing catastrophic about it. The photograph of a thing is quite capable of having no relationship to the thing itself. Just as an utterance about something concrete could be talking about something altogether different.

There was nowhere to smoke in this office. My iced coffee had melted but it didn't create more coffee. "Our editors," the title page proclaims, "include some of the leading figures of New York's art scene."

Can you guess when Betsy arrived?

THE WHEEL OF THE HOUSE

It begins with a trailer: arrows flying, men on horseback, eagles soaring through azure skies, and all the rest, right out of Fenimore Cooper, then advertisements on subway walls, and children's dreams. Gradually the narrative loses its way: there's a street, slanting snow, a low sky. When my luck changes we can name it: Petersburg.

Let's light the magic lantern, let's pass the hundredth video camera along, let's raise the blinds of a computer store in order to hear how softly the word "winchester" (as hard drives are called, in Russia) can be pronounced and immediately take leave of advanced technology in order to open up the dictionary.

"Winch," the Merriam-Webster ictionary tells us, is a "roller" or "reel," that is to say something that must be turned or wound—something that returns by its own power back to its starting point. In other words: an ordinary wheel, or from another angle: the wheel of fate (let's agree not to call it the dharma wheel). We should keep this in mind before adding the letters that make the word "winchester."

Winchester has ten letters. Between the letters are gaps. From these gaps come what we subsequently call meaning. At home, for example, these gaps sometimes take the form of raindrops unexpectedly coming through a window, of a barely discerned murmur heard through a wall at night, of a letter that describes a meeting with some melancholy-looking chess master in a pair of sunglasses long out of fashion, of the moans of lovers and stairwells.

Several stories fit into these nine, self-revelatory gaps. Their meaning is strange, in part mysterious. Each reduces some of the reliability of the other while simultaneously adding new dimensions that make it possible to overcome the one-dimensionality of conclusions and to imagine an occurrence (*sluchai*) as an intersection of a multiplicity of coordinates, which does not, however, deprive the accidental (*sluchainost*) of the attributes of divine irresponsibility.

The first of these stories (this order, without doubt, is arbitrary) is useful in that it allows itself to be told. It's the story of the building of a house. This story, which essentially coincides with a life, is nothing less than an epic tale, that is to say many intertwined stories forming a single, predestined channel in which the end of each takes us back to its origin. And in addition: back to our bewilderment.

One of them concerns New Haven, Connecticut, where in 1857 Oliver Fisher Winchester (henceforth to be called Winchester) quits a boring job in a men's shirt mill to set up a factory for the production of automatic rifles (in fact, this kind of rifle appears to have been invented by someone named V. T. Henry, but a "gap" is a gap and we can only guess why it's pronounced "in one way" and written another). The rifle is patented and played no small role in the War Between the States.

While time does its work of effacing the tracks gone with the wind and with the Winchester, we ourselves will take a peek at the confluence of these disparate episodes from a different point of view. From the point of view of Sarah Pardee. In my mind's eye I see something akin to that well-known picture of Edna St. Vincent Millay: spring mist, a flowering apple tree.

In 1858, at age eighteen, Sarah Pardee married William Winchester, son of Oliver Winchester. A few years later, after the sudden deaths of her infant daughter and, soon afterwards, her husband, Sarah Pardee came to the conclusion that the souls of those killed by the Winchester rifle (among their vast numbers were, necessarily, many American Indians) had not only taken her daughter and husband from her but were now coming back for her.

It was in Boston, during a meeting with a female medium, that this revelation from her imagination took more palpable form. There are no accounts extant of the details of their conversation. It can, however, be inferred that the medium not only confirmed Sarah Pardee's conjecture concerning the pitiless and indomitable nature of the spirits, but also explained that there was a way out of the situation.

What form did this way out take for Sarah Pardee?

In order to avoid becoming the property of bloodthirsty and vengeful demons, she would have to (according to the recommendation of the clairvoyant) begin building a house, and this construction would have to go on eternally, ceasing neither day nor night; yet if these conditions (i.e., the never-ending construction) were fulfilled, Sarah Pardee's life would also surrender those boundaries so dear to human reason.

In passing, by the way, out of the corner of an eye, just like that, even some small detail—and suddenly it's clear how everything always coincides so perfectly! Sarah Pardee received a twenty million dollar inheritance and a tax-free, daily stipend of one thousand dollars. She moved from Connecticut to the Santa Clara Valley (it's not clear why: it was a wasteland, tumbleweeds everywhere) and bought an eight-room cottage that she immediately set down to renovating. We will not describe how the "original" looked.

The "reconstruction" lasted until her death, which didn't occur until 1922. *Note:* Llanda Villa (once again, we don't know why the house was named this), which comprises 160 rooms (some assert that before the 1906 earthquake there were 708 of them), is a work that has nothing in common with what is called "architecture," i.e., with anything approximating a "plan." This resistance to what the term architecture implies ("containing a high degree of system, structure, or order") is a function of its very conception. Lacking its most important ingredient—*wholeness, completion, entirety*—Llanda Villa is, to an amazing degree, a project *contradictio in adjecto*.

This house-as-process, wavering like smoke in the imagination, became a never-ending epistle to the spirits and demons, a missive abounding in intricate allegories, crafty displacements of meaning, ellipses. Together with that, the architectural strategy itself changed during the process of construction.

We do not know exactly when an important decision—whose meaning can be reduced to the following—was made: if there really are evil spirits, then there must also be friendly spirits. And thanks to this "doubling" or division, the construction was governed not only by the need to create an invisible or frightening labyrinth, but also spaces in which friendly spirits could take shelter. It's not even out of the realm of possibility that fatigue had done its work, making Sarah Pardee feel a consequent need for allies or even just some friendly counsel.

Perhaps this explains the house's lack of mirrors. It is no secret that the most complex and terrifying labyrinth of all is the mirror. Nevertheless, according to legend, the house does indeed have two mirrors, although finding them is almost impossible since they are so-called "roving mirrors." In the Orient it is believed that such mirrors appear during séances, revealing a world of perfect symmetry to the viewer. Let's agree that the word "almost" leaves some room for hope. On the other hand, staircases ascending nowhere and then descending, or rising to the ceiling and ending there, doors (sometimes so small that only a doll could fit through them) opening onto walls, stairs with risers only two inches tall (the spirits must have gotten tired out on them), unexpected and irrelevant grill-work: these leave no hope of returning to the spot from which one departed. The wheel of the house turns unceasingly.

In the interest of full disclosure we should add several other features: columns installed upside down, the number thirteen embedded everywhere—thirteen palm trees, thirteen windows in the indoor winter garden, thirteen openings in the bathtub drains. As the poet John Ashbery writes: "The grandiosity of 'paper buildings' like Brueghel's tower of Babel, Boullée's funerary temples, Piranesi's prisons, or Sant'Elia's Futurist power stations have been realized, and by an amateur, a fanatically motivated little lady from New Haven whose dream palace was crafted with Yankee ingenuity."

I am not inclined to share Ashbery's opinion on this last point. At times it is neither sleep nor dreams that move us to actions that have seemingly no basis but which nevertheless gradually change the shape of the past and the direction of the future.

It often happens in life that we experience something that fails to take intelligible form in consciousness, it disappears without a trace and our subsequent search for it can best be defined as an endless effort to recall some kind of tormentingly necessary but unreachable memory.

I believe that for Sarah Pardee, the house was, in some sense, just such a path, an attempt to reach the memory of a memory, the secret of which was perhaps revealed to her only after death.

Nevertheless, I am still disturbed by one question: did Jorge Luis Borges know about Llanda Villa when he wrote his short story "The Immortal"? Yet even while asking this question I know that, whatever the answer, it changes nothing about the story of the wheel, the rifle, love, and an endless letter to demonic spirits.

AT THE EDGE OF THE MAGHREB

> The next night he did not know where he was, did not feel the cold. The wind blew along the ground into his mouth as he sang.
> Paul Bowles, *The Delicate Prey*

Not a Real Poet

Does it matter to whom Gertrude Stein said that he wasn't a "real poet" and not an "authentic writer"? It is well known that she was more than willing to change her point of view depending on the conditions and requirements of "the laws of composition." In any case, what interests us here is not so much Gertrude Stein's literary passions as the fact that after this pronouncement and the "recommendation" that followed, the young composer—for in the 1920s Paul Bowles considered himself a composer—felt relieved: he owed no one anything and time opened up its gateway of dreams for him. Coincidences depend not so much on desire as on the density of existence.

Every voyage is a dream. We take as many of them as needed in order to build the circular maps of our movement, backwards, to "our own beginning." One can only guess why and when Tangiers became for Paul Bowles that double point of arrival at the edge of the Maghreb, that point B, in which the role of *the other* was made irrevocably his, but not without charge, and where two cultures, Europe's and Africa's, merged at the terrestrial rupture that is Gibraltar.

It's something like a conventional hallucination, on whose stage the pleasure of intentional non-being is performed. This kind of hallucination is transparent, unemotional, and similar to lilacs, which promise to reveal the secrets of transformation to those who are patient.

Bowles's readers can, if they wish, note that the qualities I've just briefly listed are also inherent in his work: his writing is fed on a disinclination to speak, his style more effaced than impoverished.

Alcheringa

In about 1973, Paul Bowles published a kind of short essay in which he described his creative method or, more exactly, the geography of his style, a space of reading which clearly does not coincide with the scene on the page and that creates the impression of an endless approach to understanding, which is simultaneously a withdrawal from it. One gets the feeling that something other than the reader's participation is called for. However, let us dare ask the following question as we gnaw our bewildered fingers and write into the corners of our eyes with perplexed needles: why is the novel *The Sheltering Sky* (which, by the way, made it onto the celebrated list of 100 Best English-Language Novels of the Twentieth Century) translated in Russian as a combined effect of "desert, heat, flame, sand," and wandering "English patients." And yet perhaps the death of our civilization is secreted in just these kinds of images.

Let us listen to Bowles himself: "Moroccan kif-smokers like to speak of 'two worlds,' the one ruled by inexorable natural laws, and the other, the kif world, in which each person perceives 'reality' according to the projections of his own essence, the state of consciousness in which the elements of the physical universe are automatically rearranged by cannabis to suit the requirements of the individual. These distorted variations in themselves generally are of scant interest to anyone but the subject at the time he is experiencing them. An intelligent smoker, nevertheless, can aid in directing the process of deformation in such a way that the results will have value to him in his daily life. If he has faith in the accuracy of his interpretations, he will accept them as decisive, and use them to determine a subsequent plan of action. Thus, for a dedicated smoker, the passage to the 'other' world is often a pilgrimage undertaken for the express purpose of oracular consultation."

Bowles writes of just such barely noticed passages—from one waking world to another waking world—in his short story "A Thousand Days for Mokhtar."

Noise

If for Maurice Blanchot noise emerges with the death of the last author (because the author is the final authority keeping silence in the world), then for Mokhtar this authority was his wife (his bride?), whose death causes the surrounding world to be filled with a noise of ever-growing and inexorable power. Mokhtar has a dream in which he kills a friend at the village market. Upon awakening he goes to the market and, in the middle of an unexpected argument over a debt that has supposedly not been repaid, Mokhtar realizes that he does not want the murder to take place. He says: "Last night I dreamed that I came here and killed this man, who is my friend. I do not want to kill him. I am not going to kill him. Look carefully. I am not hurting him."

Then the murder takes place. In the penultimate episode the judge addresses Mokhtar:

> "I have heard from the witnesses what happened in the market," said the Qadi impatiently, "and from those same witnesses I know you are an evil man. It is impossible for the mind of an upright man to bring forth an evil dream. Bouchta died as a result of your dream." And as Mokhtar attempted to interrupt: "I know what you are going to say, but you are a fool, Mokhtar. You blame the wind, the night,

your long solitude. Good. For a thousand days in our prison here you will not hear the wind, you will not know whether it is night or day, and you will never lack the companionship of your fellow prisoners."

Nothing special. It even provides the obligatory false signal—*in the silence of prison* Mokhtar remembers that he really did owe his friend the money and that the latter had a perfect right to reproach him for it. A perfectly literary short story. Narrated with complete clarity. But whether the story coincides with its meaning is another question. The things of the given world are unchangeable. They are what they are. At dawn a shard of rock-face appears to be the head of an old man, at dusk we notice that we are gazing on the outline of a hand. The gradual change of color, of intensity, outline, of point of view, the vagaries of indigestion, some unintentionally received information, a book fallen on the floor—all this, and many other things, are "passages." Each object knows where the source of vision lies.

But in the space between the expected and what potentially exists outside of all perception and experience gleams a "third," the "coexistent condition" and its expression—"an expression," as Werner Heisenberg has written, "with an interim significance of meaning that cannot be expressed in everyday language."

Paul Bowles came into this world on December 30, 1910 in New York.

He Who Enters, Exits
As a young man Bowles wrote a short story called "The Frozen Fields," about a young boy who dreams of having a friendship with a wolf who seizes his father by the throat and carries him off. It is hard to

say whether this story is evidence of Bowles's tense relationship with his father or his acquaintance with the legend of Pankeev. Certainly literature doesn't lack for fairy tales about wolves. There's no mention of the subject in any of his letters. However, in one, dated September 18, 1958, and written to a publisher eager for biographical information, Bowles does give a detailed description of the trajectory of his "passage." He explains that he was born in New York and grew up during Prohibition. Having completed secondary school at age sixteen, he enrolled at an art school. Quickly finding painting "silly," he transferred to the University of Virginia, "because Poe went there." After a semester he left Virginia and went to Paris, where he had already managed to get published in several literary magazines.

He got bored with Paris incredibly fast. He wandered around Europe for a time, then returned to America and the university, quit again, then went back to Paris. Apparently it was at this time that he met Gertrude Stein, was informed that he wasn't a "real" poet, and that he'd be better off heading to Morocco.

Then came Algiers, the Sahara, the West Indies, South America, Mexico (four years). In between he returned to New York and wrote scores for Broadway shows, "including among them the first William Saroyan play and the first Tennessee Williams play . . . Then I went down to the Sahara and wrote *The Sheltering Sky.*"

Sixteen years after his first visit to Morocco, he moved to Tangiers, where he established himself permanently. Together with his wife Jane. Their marriage has been the subject of numerous commentaries.

In the 1950s William Burroughs took refuge from his troubles there in Tangiers. His book *Interzone* tells a lot about the Tangier of that time. After Burroughs, it was Allen Ginsberg's turn to hang out there. Exactly who else came and went during those years is not known. In his diary John Hopkins mentions many names: Barbara Hutton, Brian Gysin, Princess Ruspoli, Malcolm Forbes, Timothy Leary, Estelle Parsons, J. Paul Getty, Rudolf Nureyev, Yves Saint-Laurent . . .

The Other Side of the Moon

It wavers before me, this mirage, and I can't shake it; sometimes it's as though someone else's wearisome memory or premonition has taken insistent hold of me. I see the deck of a ship, I even seem to catch the scent of burning wood, of tar, salt, and turquoise; and then I see *them,* seated in lawn chairs or standing by launches, frozen in the water's reflected light, holding their hats against the wind—in other words, the transatlantic era. The dark sun of Okeanos shines down from all sides. Writing, I repeat (I must not lose sight of this), means dooming oneself to eternal tardiness in full knowledge that any story, even the most complicated one, even one filled with trembling, ecstasy, and horror, will end in a tautology, with a metallic taste in one's mouth and a bitter burning in the eyes. The writer dreams of night while being sentenced to an omnipotent and eternal dawn, when even the banality of a shadow can't relieve the impersonal nothingness of his surroundings.

1984, Leningrad, Mechnikov Prospekt. To my complete surprise I've been sent two boxes of books by John Martin, the publisher of Black Sparrow Press. Among the tomes of Wyndam Lewis, John Wieners, Charles Olson, etc., there turns out to be two novels of Paul Bowles and a collection of his short stories. At present I don't have a single page of his work in my house. They all ended up at Vassily Kondratyev's, although he told me that one of them, the collected stories, was given to Sergey Khrenov for translation.

Slavoj Žižek has written that the horrifying impression made by underwater photographs of the *Titanic* is not a result of their symbolic over-determination, their metaphoric meaning—"it is not so much a representation as an inert presence." It is—he writes—the materialization of a horrifying, impossible *pleasure:* "We find ourselves in a forbidden zone, in a site that should have remained unseen: that which has become accessible to our sight is something like a petrified forest of pleasure."

Tangerine Dream

Tangiers is one of the oldest cities in northwest Africa. Literature is one of the forms of public consciousness. Tangiers was originally inhabited by the Phoenicians. The hero of a literary work expresses what is most typical of his time. The Carthaginians drove out the Phoenicians, and the city was later taken by Rome. Russia is a kind of hallucination. There is no such thing as a "passage." The term *thanatos* does not appear in the works of Freud; however, according to his biographer Jones, Freud did make use of the word in speech. The Arabs took Tangiers in 705, but did not make it part of the Ottoman Empire. Portugal ruled it in 1471; in 1923 it was made part of the international zone. The river Mao has its source in Tangiers, then turns east and empties into Lake In. There are many horses of a kind called *bo*. They have a white coat, a single horn, and a tail like an ox. Their whinny sounds like a human scream. When mandarin oranges began to be sold in Tangiers, their name was changed to tangerine.

Surely some of us still remember the band Tangerine Dream. On December 10, 1999, in the Italian Hospital in Tangiers, which is located close to the site in which the film *Casablanca* takes place, Paul Bowles died.

WEEKDAYS

Professor V. Savchuk
9/21/00
19:17:03

Dear V. V. S.,

I'm on the ninth floor, which as you know is a lucky number and was of service to the beautiful Beatrice.

I live on Washington Place, which is actually a tiny alley, a kind of park in the middle of Manhattan, between Washington Square and Broadway itself. The building seems to be a pre-war construction, probably from the 1930s, fifteen stories high and permeated from top to bottom with the glass canals of pneumatic mail tubes: just to look at them, even in passing, immediately transports the soul to that strange era of literary scandals, publishers' soirées, and transatlantic cruises. The transom of my apartment window—the window covers the entire wall—is made of several strips of thinly plaited cast iron. In its quality of sound this street suggests a Stradivarius—even the most indistinctly murmured word, uttered somewhere down below, echoes and re-echoes throughout my room. Polyphony, it would seem, is inherent not only to poetry.

The immediate area around the building is considered part of the campus. Indeed, the local police are not referred to by the usual term, *security,* but rather *protection.* You'll have to agree that, although small, there's a real semantic difference there.

It's a forty-second walk from my apartment to work. In the rain I don't even have time to open an umbrella. My office opens directly onto Broadway. The traffic light on the corner has been decorated by a local artist with bits of broken coffee cups. Very colorful, and they'll be there till the Second Coming. The classes I teach are held in two different buildings: Tish Hall, a vast, although not especially tall, terra-cotta structure (fifteen stories, not counting three underground floors), and in the main building of the School of Arts and Sciences. Sixth Avenue is totally mysterious. It heads north and then abruptly ends in the sky, at Central Park. It's quite possible that it was originally designed as an exit route for all the tribes of the world. It could certainly accommodate them.

The Slavic Department, which is located on the sixth floor, contains not only professors' offices but a small departmental library and administrative office, with a computer, printer, lamp, chairs and shelves, telephone, a coffee machine, and the like. There are also a series of "conference rooms" in which the classes themselves are held: the rooms are large (thirty to forty square meters), with sound-proofed walls, impressive oval tables, straight-backed chairs (all of wood), and enormous leather couches lining the walls, which must be avoided at all cost, because if you fall into their beckoning arms, all hope of surfacing again on the waves of being must be abandoned.

Three minutes away, around the corner of the hall, is Avital Ronell's office. Her door is always open. She herself is seated in front of her Mac and wearing a Chinese straw hat. The kind the coolies wore during the construction of the great California railroad. She has the habit of waving a friendly hand to passersby. By the way, one of my first days here, while I was wandering around looking for a water fountain, who should I run into but Professor Derrida (he was looking for the exit)—but he disappeared and I haven't seen him since. Nevertheless, strange things continue to happen periodically—this morning for example, walking past an office, I noticed, on the list of people signed up to meet with their faculty advisor, the name Walter Benjamin. It would be hard to anticipate what he might have wanted to talk about . . .

It's possible that I'll meet him at a party—one of those faculty parties that are like natural disasters, since they're inevitably held during the workweek. Usually they're scheduled during the first month of the semester so that we can "get to know each other better." Wine, cheese, and mineral water are served. Those are all the provisions we get for this kind of bivouac. Once, a professor in a neighboring office brought a bottle of home brew—everyone greeted the sight of it with enthusiastic exclamations, but they were afraid to actually drink the stuff.

But let's head home. Within five-minutes' walk in any direction are numerous bookstores. Feeling an irresistible need to give my eyes and brain a brief workout, I stop at a few of them on the way: how can a mind unprepared for such a quantity of books and titles stand up to the experience? I don't know where America ranks on the list of "biggest countries of readers in the world," but it seems that here even the homeless, whose numbers appear to be declining catastrophically (the grim reaper? emigration to Russia? marooned on the ocean floor by submarine? or have they just turned back into phantoms?), cart around a couple of piles of books. For two days running I've noticed one homeless fellow, on the steps of the Arts and Sciences building, with a book on the art of Mauritanian Spain. And you won't believe whom I saw a few days ago at the Grove Street Path Station: Marat Gelman. He was heading up to Rockefeller Center. Reading the instruction manual for his new mobile phone.

But that's not the subject I want to talk about, not reading, to which I've got to get used to again; no, I want to speak about the incredible semiotic saturation of this city. It would be perfectly reasonable to conceive of New York as a gigantic letter, the verso of which is turned directly toward us. To a certain extent, this is what accounts for the city's extraordinarily high level of mental and emotional saturation, making it one of a kind.

What didn't we talk about, Misha Iampolski and I, as we wandered unhurriedly among the bookstalls and bookstores between Bleeker and Mercer streets! Our conversation was like our walk itself, branching off whimsically, flitting from one subject to another, before finally focusing on the history of the relationship of Diderot and Falconet, to their fifteen-year correspondence on the subject of the eternal and the ephemeral, during which Diderot unexpectedly dropped a line about art's ability to adequately express an inner state—and it ended with these Italian words: *esse Pulcinella!*

According to Iampolski, this phrase has to do with a once well-known story about a Venetian monk. This monk, enraged by a delirious crowd that was surrounding a street Pulcinella, screamed out: "You're looking at a false Pulcinella, a pretender! The *real* Pulcinella is over there!" And he pointed toward the crucifixion.

Perhaps the monk's name was Savonarola, perhaps it was something else. History is silent on this point. As we weren't in position to resolve it, we instead took a seat at an outdoor Italian café. It was sunny and windy. I ordered espresso, Misha ordered tea.

Each day my walk gets longer, simplifying the landscape. By the way, every morning, at Union Square, which is about ten blocks north of here, the local peasants sell agricultural products. The corn is splendid, you boil it for three minutes and it's incredibly tasty—with blue cheese and wine, of course.

Soon it will be time for me to make another pilgrimage down along the shelves of Chilean wine. It will probably include the Italian and French shelves as well. There are even some very fine Spanish vintages you can find. Vino Tondonia Reserva 1993, for example, or even the august Marqués de Cáceres Rioja.

All for now.

Forever yours,
ATD

October 2000
New York

TRANSLATION BY THOMAS EPSTEIN

SAND TO SAND

Summer passed in the dried garden, with its flowering
fortunes. Most of it is now covered in its autumn coat. We
can't see what else has dried up, withered or fallen. Any-
thing that didn't fall in the spring or summer is now com-
ing down.
Leon Bogdanov

Everything is clear as day now. I wasn't in the best of moods when
I flew out. I flew out on the day of vernal equinox, on Nowrūz. My
boarding pass was number thirteen, and the plane wasn't one of the
best. My ears kept popping. Even the cognac that Arlando V. M.,
who was flying from Krakow to Petersburg, offered me at the airport
didn't help.

Then later, on the way back, the person sitting next to me, by the
window, who introduced himself as Herman (engrossed in his game
of *Sudden Strike*, adding a Raphaelesque charm to the scene with
his twelve-inch screen), having told me some detailed horror stories
about our country's aeronautic industry—which froze my blood—
promised to call me when we got home; and to my shy remark about
the different kinds of beer on offer, said:

—You're imagining things: any beer can be made first rate, but
even if they really do try to make it first rate, do everything they can,
brew it in small batches, like they used to do at home, whatever you
like, it's all the same in the end (it's just beer, after all) and conversations about good or bad beer are all just about marketing . . . Take
my advice, if you don't want to seem naïve, never say that this brand

is better or worse than the other. It's all rumors and hearsay. Forget about it . . . Every brand is made to suit everyone.

Herman turned out to be the manager of one of the beer breweries in the suburbs of Petersburg, and his imaginary suitcase was pasted all over with traveling labels and periodic misery.

The airport in Stockholm was rather mediocre. I left the painter, an acquaintance of mine, irritated, with his two carts piled with canvases (the exhibition *has already taken place*), and together with Karl Dicker set out to the August Strindberg Hotel, secretly hoping that as soon as I got there, I could look for the "Red Room," which was one of the important goals of my visit. We found the hotel after circling around the block nine times.

The three-storied building was situated in the second courtyard. There was a spiral fire-escape stairwell outside my window. Beyond the fire-escape's platform, deep night enveloped the yard. In the house across the way somebody was hunched over an empty stove in the kitchen. He stood frozen like that. I'm shortsighted. Soon, Karl and I were walking to the place where we were supposed to do our readings. One could sense the night—everywhere, even though we didn't have the properly clear sky and absence of dust that would have let us see the stars.

■

There was a faded print of Madame la Duchesse d'Holstein Gottorp on the wall. A moonless night. The reading took place in a grand café, with a crowd of about two hundred people who all sat at their tables, murmuring to each other, listening to our "verses" and asking questions. The beer stall to the right of the main stage was doing a brisk business. The staff members were drinking wine and wandering away from their stations. World Poetry Day was nearing the dawn of its end. It started snowing (like phosphor) towards morning.

Time—in the fjords. I keep wanting to go and see how time sits in the basins. Which is why I'll digress about ice floes, time lying in the holes in the fjords, and other things as well. Dried gardens, for instance. Here it is—the first digression. There are a number of memories, which, when our thoughts return to them, don't seem like such delightful encounters anymore, granting us the possibility of self-negation; though there always remains a fascination with this return, a return to an area where possibility loses its saturation and gently glimmers in clearly outlined partitions of memory, satisfied with its familiar proportions—where the holes left by absences get filled to the brim with the most minute details. I'll try to explain what I just said with an example, which, in my opinion, is well known to many, if not everyone. Sometimes even hyperbole calls for some leniency.

In any case, the phenomenon of "recreating" the past—which phrase, in this context, has the advantage over the unreliable word "memory," and which appears moreover to be more accurate a portrayal of the successive actions of our psychic mechanisms—is markedly different from those brief "flashes" of amnesia we experience when, in an inexpressibly brief instant, a particular memory undergoes countless transformations.

It's important to note here that we're not talking about those metamorphoses affected on our memories from the "outside," but transformations within a person who exposes himself to the abyss of dissolution in those incorporeal times called the "past," and simultaneously in the corporeal time of the "present," where the aperture is set to provide an illusive focus. Was it the smell of tobacco coming from the open window at dusk, after the May thunderstorm, that brought the scent of matthiola? Or is it the rustling of autumn leaves under my feet, and a razor-like patch of light reflected on a car window frozen at the corner of my pupil? Or, perhaps, a faint profile in a crowd, and also, as if tracing a dropping arch—a flat bird streaming over the turquoise sky roof, and occasionally, two–three unpretentious words on found rice paper?

Leaving poetic embellishments aside, let's ask an idle question: Do you remember the rare magnesium white projecting such displacements? The instant of "*texture gazing into texture*." Probably, yes, or else how would it be possible to have so many works about writers. Should we draw lines between them? And those who write about them. Everything can stay as is. But things don't always not stay as "is," they can disappear, leaving behind voids which seem almost familiar, and yet achieved through the comfortable familiarity of an exquisite non-conformity. Parenthetically, the Nazca Lines were revealed only at the beginning of the 1920s, when an airline was opened between Peru and Chile. All that's left from this enigmatic civilization is an eighty-five mile plateau inscribed with geoglyphs—geometrical figures, outlines of birds, lizards, and insects. The average length of each pattern is about a mile.

Having written a few paragraphs of prefatory material for Leon Bogdanov's book, forthcoming from the New Literary Review Press, I walked into a nearby 7-Eleven. My trip to get pasta and beer in the morning became the subject of a lively conversation with the doorman, and then with a garbage collector on the street, who was observing me for a long time as I took photographs of the church on the corner and who finally asked, "Are you from St. Petersburg?" To which I replied—"Yes."

How did he figure it out? Because the church was named after St. Peter, he said. Very logical. "But still, why would it even occur to you?"—I wanted to know. He answered that he had previous experience in the matter, and besides, he got up before everyone else and commuted to Stockholm, one-and-a-half hours each way.

Last night, I told him, a black man behind the 7-Eleven asked me, "How long have you been here from the Bronx?" I said I was from the Kalininsky District, you know, where Mechnikov Hospital is. He nodded and asked: "What about Pesach?" I told him I wasn't Jewish, but that, as far as I knew, everything was the same as ever with Passover. At which he pointed his thumb to his chest and said that he wasn't Jewish either, but when everyone's together, it always turns out *almost* the other way around. The garbage collector said that he knew well what that "almost" meant—that he wasn't Swedish but Norwegian—but really, things weren't so simple. Anyway, everything was different during summer, he added. It's the season when all the rats come out. Rats with long tails.

Dear Leon, I didn't see the rats, but I saw Hans Bjorkegren: he's handsome, like a noble patrician engraved on a coin lost in the black ground on the Ides of March. Wine from cardboard boxes. Cobblestones underfoot. Fog on the edge of a blade—more about this later, and in whisper. Traces of my feet on the windowsill. Somewhere in Egypt, on one of the palimpsests of a papyrus boat, on one of the *R*s from a name that's no longer popular . . . Ask me what I wanted to see in Stockholm. Whether I knocked at the door to get the letters from . . . ?

I saw Leon Bogdanov only once, many years ago. I wouldn't argue if someone insisted it was in November. In reality, it was a month that didn't by nature exclude the possibility of being set in a different year entirely—it all happened in a way that's really hard to recall. A shadow crossing a face. Flying devices, ropes, acrobats, people in the audience—dissolving from the realization that they are engaged in something that's never existed (what they'll try to describe scrupulously in every possible publication, proving just the opposite).

We didn't want to drink vodka but we did. We ate ice cream because everything else was more expensive than tea. Back then, the future was already taking a hold of us in that precious state of idleness. I was indifferent to the future, like I was to names. It would be other people who'd write about this, not us, because we still had time for other things—hence the proximity of the fjords. But I was happy, although nothing stirred in me. Because it all happened as though he came to my room on Tegnergatan at 7:00 A.M. Where the subject of time arose at daybreak—but let's leave that for another digression. However, I did ask. They told me that he never stayed here. I was looking at the door from the spiral stairwell; the one on the wall outside, sadly not Escherian. Then tell me, where could he have possibly stayed?

I saw the same sloped streets in cobblestone, with which dreams are paved. From where nobody finds their way home again. I knew that I was going to stay at the Strindberg. The Scandinavian tiger leaps from children's maps, leaving dust behind on the meridians. But who knew that August S. liked beer more than anything and wanted to be a butterfly? Was this a surprise when I drove up to the uninviting coaching inn, which leads to one thing—Arlando.

I knew that I was going to stay at the Strindberg. The Scandinavian tiger leaps from children's maps, leaving behind dust on the meridians. But who knew that August Strindberg liked beer and butterflies more than anything else? Was it a surprise when I drove into the bleak coaching inn? It's impossible to fall out. Everything is on the same level. And the rail(line)roads stretch out of your sleeve. The panorama of the central station unfolds three steps from Madame la Duchesse d'Holstein. I'm interested in something else—all of the "invisible" patterns that were there for more than four thousand years, as Eliot Weinberger writes, were created during the process of fragmentation and withdrawal of the surface layer, the dark oxidized soil, underneath which was a lighter stone substrate. Was this a demonstration of their knowledge of mineralogy? Geology? Simply tectonic movements, whose patterns eventually merged into mystical forms? What about time? Was it "stored away" by monstrously slow processes such as oxidation or erosion? Or the cultivation of Beaujolais? Or moving from Vasilevsky Island to Zamshin Street? I'm talking about a strange book about the desert. It's as though we were watching ourselves unpack, throughout time. When, in the opinion of one philosopher, "the present disappears in its own light."

Sure, I'm interested in other things, but nobody will write about Leon Bogdanov. Nobody will do it because they don't understand how to "store themselves away" in plaster gauze that would bring them closer to the borderline, where he didn't want to exist *at all*, as this was a given condition in his name: *Bogdanov*, "given by God."

Leon Bogdanov appeared at a time when I least expected him to. Which is why today, in Scandinavia, the land that leaps out from bottomless coloring maps and where the "hangman" and "mother" coincide in the square of a transatlantic fracture, I return to him.

This is the same as going against the wind. He emerges similar to the imperfectly tailored orthography of French prose, but belongs to those fabulous times when everybody, except for us, thought that writing meant, if not to reveal a mystery, then, in the worst case, at least to say that the mystery was inevitable. Habits, Bogdanov wrote, don't exist. God is not a habit. In order to see light at a certain angle, it's necessary to avert it to the opposite side of its axis. Almost all of Paul Klee's work is a silent journey towards the yantra. Towards a reversed perspective. The blade is nothing but a process of reducing a concrete material body to nothingness, "*from which all creative expressions were made by expansion of the point of mysterious brightness.*" Does the light help us to see? It can be presumed, also, that two provisionally selected perspectives can coexist together. Besides, there's no basis for doubting that the desire to control a similar state will never leave us. For his own salvation: he *existed* through disappearance. I could be stoned for this. They'll say: he always wanted to *be*. But didn't he get lost in the horizon of writing like a rabbit in a magician's hat, and isn't that the proof of my statement?

The most important and terrible plant in his dried garden, I repeat, was the wind caught in the balcony door. Leon Bogdanov *was* the continuous process of the *constantly* creating blade, with which he could dissect any "stories." Does the one who inhales realize that somebody else will breathe in his exhalation? So it's necessary to gather your breath slowly and not rush in with vertigo. Heidegger is resting. A blade that's cutting itself. A few quotes from Bogdanov. They don't leave the possibility of a "third," which is supposedly given. They bear witness to what is always given only once. He himself was Periegetes of his own *zemlia* or "earth" (a word that could have the following possible etymological roots: *za*—"beyond" + *emlit*—"taking" = *zaemlit*—"appropriate"), or in other words, a place where "possessing oneself" is renounced. But not the earth, nor the sky, nor even myself. Nothing is given. "Where should we search for a borderline between the valuable and insignificant, big and small? Outside of things or inside of them?"—asked Khebo.

But that's not right either. He's nothing like Rozanov. Sunk in his iron boots up to his neck—Bogdanov never wanted to be like him. That's why I froze to death once reading a poem by Elena Fanailova about winter in a bus. How to learn not to loosen your strings, hands, keys . . . imagination? No, he's nothing like Beckett, Musil, or Kenko Hoshi. Here's the main thing. He looked at the map, propping it against the window, against wax, against the wing of a bird—which is why the castle, the village, and the guards—including the "gates"— are only modest stations for the moving eye. Which is why the critic can't see him.

My intention here is quite obvious; a traveler on the northern border of oleography. Without palm trees, Lermontov, or profits, but "at work" with a cigarette in my hand. Coming from everywhere. Coming like the science of water and rust come together in a textbook. *Almost* now. Which also means: the nonexistence of location. Read Leon Bogdanov and write a preface. Or better yet, write as Bogdanov wrote. Which is ridiculously simple. Some words, in some kind of sequence, well . . . perhaps a little patience, too. Right now, I'm trying to do what Bogdanov didn't do.

Literary truth is actually made up of the endless selection and separation of one from the other. Presumably, for the salvation of those who *separate* and possibly for some other reason as well. Maybe—to give a recipe from death. But who's arguing anyway? The last sweet morsel falls under the philosopher's tooth. But each tooth has its own dentist, who chants—"Don't go inside the root, go through the canal."

The canal is what we call "pluralities," which come close to Klee's paintings. "The angel" stolen from Benjamin and bridges suspended in the air. Ruins. Dentists have created webs, but not earthquakes. Neither for me, nor for Bogdanov. The circles are narrowing, as after gentle tectonic displacements. Bogdanov emerges in the background of a Kantian *chanson* on absolute space. But this, too, isn't interesting at the end of the day in a country where the same children walk on empty streets. And so I return to the beginning of my remarks. About memory, flashes of its absence. About poets, who leave their verses anywhere. Tyutchev's verses rolled up after the State Council meeting. Who found them?—I forget. The verses Khodasevich left under a tree. Then it rained. Someone picked them up. They were saved. This doesn't mean that I like Khodasevich's poetry. I, for example, don't like the proof of theorem X, because something else is left over that I don't like either. Who is left?—That's another question. But how else should we look at things?

P.S.
I need to remind myself that this isn't the best "work" of its kind: nine hours of writing, a hamburger, about 18,000 typed characters by morning, a bottle of Chilean Santa Digna from the Miguel Torres winery, three bottles of warm Tuborg (and who wants to count the cigarette butts?).

I'm finishing this like a woodpecker working on a tree—Friday,

March 22, 2002. The August Strindberg Hotel. In the apertures of time, I'm revising my future book, which will be called *Dust*. I can't get through to Zina, Ostap's MTS won't connect. Wanted to buy a phone card and make a few calls—wasn't able to. "We don't carry those anymore, everyone's using cell phones now," etc. . . .

It's more likely that, to a certain degree, this text changes our relation to simple things—namely, "I," and then "everything else"—indeed, this should be more evident than ever out in the world. This dichotomy will never become one. Otherwise, I have a feeling that nobody would ever find out about the existence of such vain little contradictions and similarities. Hence the question: *what* is a work? Just try to close the bracket.

TRANSLATION BY ANA LUCIC & SHUSHAN AVAGYAN

Many things are gone, they ceased to exist long before vanishing into oblivion. Things like faces, names, words, and also a pair of scissors lost last summer, as well as a few books, the fate of which is still a mystery to this day. Unimpeded, impatience lapses into indifference, making it impossible to distinguish one from the other. According to dictionaries, "monumentality" is derived from the concentration of power apparatuses—such as military forces, wealth, intelligence services, universities, and industries—into one locus. Cemeteries can certainly be included in that list. Benjamin's image of the angel of history, searching (in the wind) among the sprouting ruins of greatness, nonetheless found its place in the configuration of meanings.

The wind has no sense of "there"; the angel's face is darkened with the shadows of "fuzzy set" theory. Petersburg has no sense of "here," which is why it's pointless to talk about its limits.

But there are other horizontal axes around which the points of "not here" and "not there" have been randomly scattered. Michel Serres calls them *hors-là*. To me, these are points that transition into the *other*: they are exploratory, four-dimensional corpuscles of a *beyond-darkness*.

The only thing that remains unchanged in this city is the light. It can't ever be replaced with any reflection or dimension. Vision has abandoned all attempts to connect it to color, size, form . . . And I should say—me too. After all, I didn't learn anything about the "other." Time has excluded him from his personal narrative.

The deserted centuries don't remind me of anything. Love doesn't cede to time. Streaming from a slanted angle, rushing to become one with the shadow, moving and motionless, connecting the day with the night with a promise of an irrevocable silence—like illuminations in old manuscripts covered with fragile sheets of papyrus—the light mesmerizes, like water, and its ripples, that convulse like arteries pulsating with blood, move relentlessly in shafts of busy molecules, particles of its surroundings.

This is exactly how it was in the beginning. Streets, links, messages. On each corner. I have no reason not to believe you. The optics of equinox and equidistance—a monstrously slow flash of something traceless, or the sun rising over the city.

Sometimes it feels like floating between layers of mercury and ice.

Comparisons, however, get old and inadequate as the pure form of description yields itself to anticipation. It's probably the evaporating light and anticipation that produce these outlines that we so easily guess are the shapes of conjecture, rain, possibility, speculation, and philosophy.

And sometimes the eye catches something altogether unimaginable—for example, a reproduction of the *Villa la Mouette* by Edwin Dickinson.

TRANSLATION BY EVGENY PAVLOV

DUST

It's easy to get accustomed to a wealthy lifestyle. It's much harder to forget poverty.

Everything around seemed so real that one wanted desperately to wake up.

There's nothing more unexciting than conversations of writers about literature, women about love, actors about theater, or politicians about their good intentions. Everything becomes dull when its existence is forced by necessity.

Aporia, motto, paradox, etc.—a condition of thought where the answer continually outstrips the question.

In the end, pleasure turns out to be something that excludes happiness, the labor to experience joy, a redundancy of knowledge, and so on.

When I hear "You should work" from a person, whose eyes project the uncertain melancholy of an idiot, I realize that my idleness is lost virtue.

Levels of comprehension stretch beyond the borders of difference between, for example, vodka and wine, wine and beer, beer and water, water and sand. This is where the difference between "sex" and "conversations about sex" fades away, leaving some light residue of disappointment.

We talk only because of a persistent desire to understand what is it that we are saying. As a result, we allow ourselves to speculate that, all in all, we have fallen, by chance, into a distorted phrase—"here and now"—the "correctness" of which, when uttered repeatedly, depends on *how* we disappear into it.

Surprisingly, there are very few clouds today.

War eclipses death. When a person loses his "constancy of reason," he resorts to glorifying war or inventing "traditions," "songs," and the "past."

However, to a certain degree, war has always been the most straightforward way of illustrating death (in a quantitative sense). So we could say that war is one of the ways to study death from a different perspective, beyond the limits of literature. What an inarticulate metaphor! It's probably better to say: there are more clouds today than usual.

Old age is marked by a somewhat stronger (than previously) attraction to the word "soul." The dream of reason generates metaphors.

Death (in any implication of this meaningless word) implies the application of an absolutely pure language.

Those whose minds turn constantly to the *desert* (Paul Bowles, for example, not to go too far), or those who get the shivers just picturing it, must feel awkward and out of place among those who eagerly "experience" immortality in theory.

Many people have gone mad, without even realizing it, in an attempt to connect their image (in the mirror or photograph) with *themselves*. In the disruption between "oneself" and "self" in/on the image, the mind loses its habits of recognizing its own presence. Insomnia is capable of prolonging only a chain of comparisons.

Even today I get the most pleasure from lying in a hammock with a book, gazing beyond its pages. This applies to my own writing as well. And when I write this, I see certain things, which haven't changed in forty years—for example, the big old linden tree, or sunshine under my eyelids.

At first, the thought of the sheer quantity of what's been written by others is disturbing, but it's also slightly exciting. Then excitement turns into irritation. Over the course of years you start to feel dread that gradually evolves into irony and, finally, into tedium. Obviously, all conversations about "good" and "bad" in this context are inappropriate.

Philosophy can somehow seem impressive—with its, we'll say, uncontainable nature that always comes to the same conclusion about its own contradictions. This realization is doubtlessly an impulse for its next scenario. Which, in fact, favorably distinguishes it from all other genres.

No, after all it's not the frequency with which we use the word "soul" that signals the approach of old age, but the indifference of the hand holding the telephone receiver.

This weakness crosses out the time and space of the Other with an authoritative and irrevocable hand.

"I'll send you another postcard with a biplane. Or most likely a Gillespie vintage 'aeroplane,' though 'biplane' sounds better, if you, of course, remember what a biplane looks like from your post-war childhood.

The Gillespie Aeroplane, 1905.

This plane is remarkable because, according to the postcard, it 'preserves an equilibrium' and allows the pilot to be the 'active agent'—meaning, it's made so that the pilot has full control with the help of steel cables . . ." (2000, Turin).

It took Margaret Meklina and me a whole year to write *A Year of Correspondence*. A year later Mitya decided to publish it.

It warmed up towards the evening. Then it started to snow. But it was a different evening.

TRANSLATION BY ANA LUCIC & SHUSHAN AVAGYAN

PETROS ABATZOGLOU, *What Does Mrs. Freeman Want?*
PIERRE ALBERT-BIROT, *Grabinoulor.*
YUZ ALESHKOVSKY, *Kangaroo.*
FELIPE ALFAU, *Chromos.*
　Locos.
IVAN ÂNGELO, *The Celebration.*
　The Tower of Glass.
DAVID ANTIN, *Talking.*
ANTÓNIO LOBO ANTUNES, *Knowledge of Hell.*
ALAIN ARIAS-MISSON, *Theatre of Incest.*
JOHN ASHBERY AND JAMES SCHUYLER, *A Nest of Ninnies.*
DJUNA BARNES, *Ladies Almanack.*
　Ryder.
JOHN BARTH, *LETTERS.*
　Sabbatical.
DONALD BARTHELME, *The King.*
　Paradise.
SVETISLAV BASARA, *Chinese Letter.*
MARK BINELLI, *Sacco and Vanzetti Must Die!*
ANDREI BITOV, *Pushkin House.*
LOUIS PAUL BOON, *Chapel Road.*
　Summer in Termuren.
ROGER BOYLAN, *Killoyle.*
IGNÁCIO DE LOYOLA BRANDÃO, *Teeth under the Sun.*
　Zero.
BONNIE BREMSER, *Troia: Mexican Memoirs.*
CHRISTINE BROOKE-ROSE, *Amalgamemnon.*
BRIGID BROPHY, *In Transit.*
MEREDITH BROSNAN, *Mr. Dynamite.*
GERALD L. BRUNS,
　Modern Poetry and the Idea of Language.
EVGENY BUNIMOVICH AND J. KATES, EDS.,
　Contemporary Russian Poetry: An Anthology.
GABRIELLE BURTON, *Heartbreak Hotel.*
MICHEL BUTOR, *Degrees.*
　Mobile.
　Portrait of the Artist as a Young Ape.
G. CABRERA INFANTE, *Infante's Inferno.*
　Three Trapped Tigers.
JULIETA CAMPOS, *The Fear of Losing Eurydice.*
ANNE CARSON, *Eros the Bittersweet.*
CAMILO JOSÉ CELA, *Christ versus Arizona.*
　The Family of Pascual Duarte.
　The Hive.
LOUIS-FERDINAND CÉLINE, *Castle to Castle.*
　Conversations with Professor Y.
　London Bridge.
　North.
　Rigadoon.
HUGO CHARTERIS, *The Tide Is Right.*
JEROME CHARYN, *The Tar Baby.*
MARC CHOLODENKO, *Mordechai Schamz.*
EMILY HOLMES COLEMAN, *The Shutter of Snow.*
ROBERT COOVER, *A Night at the Movies.*
STANLEY CRAWFORD, *Log of the S.S. The Mrs Unguentine.*
　Some Instructions to My Wife.
ROBERT CREELEY, *Collected Prose.*
RENÉ CREVEL, *Putting My Foot in It.*
RALPH CUSACK, *Cadenza.*
SUSAN DAITCH, *L.C.*
　Storytown.
NICHOLAS DELBANCO, *The Count of Concord.*
NIGEL DENNIS, *Cards of Identity.*
PETER DIMOCK,
　A Short Rhetoric for Leaving the Family.
ARIEL DORFMAN, *Konfidenz.*
COLEMAN DOWELL, *The Houses of Children.*
　Island People.
　Too Much Flesh and Jabez.
ARKADII DRAGOMOSHCHENKO, *Dust.*
RIKKI DUCORNET, *The Complete Butcher's Tales.*
　The Fountains of Neptune.
　The Jade Cabinet.
　The One Marvelous Thing.
　Phosphor in Dreamland.
　The Stain.
　The Word "Desire."
WILLIAM EASTLAKE, *The Bamboo Bed.*
　Castle Keep.
　Lyric of the Circle Heart.
JEAN ECHENOZ, *Chopin's Move.*
STANLEY ELKIN, *A Bad Man.*
　Boswell: A Modern Comedy.
　Criers and Kibitzers, Kibitzers and Criers.
　The Dick Gibson Show.
　The Franchiser.
　George Mills.
　The Living End.
　The MacGuffin.
　The Magic Kingdom.
　Mrs. Ted Bliss.
　The Rabbi of Lud.
　Van Gogh's Room at Arles.
ANNIE ERNAUX, *Cleaned Out.*

LAUREN FAIRBANKS, *Muzzle Thyself.*
　Sister Carrie.
LESLIE A. FIEDLER, *Love and Death in the American Novel.*
GUSTAVE FLAUBERT, *Bouvard and Pécuchet.*
KASS FLEISHER, *Talking out of School.*
FORD MADOX FORD, *The March of Literature.*
JON FOSSE, *Melancholy.*
MAX FRISCH, *I'm Not Stiller.*
　Man in the Holocene.
CARLOS FUENTES, *Christopher Unborn.*
　Distant Relations.
　Terra Nostra.
　Where the Air Is Clear.
JANICE GALLOWAY, *Foreign Parts.*
　The Trick Is to Keep Breathing.
WILLIAM H. GASS, *Cartesian Sonata and Other Novellas.*
　A Temple of Texts.
　The Tunnel.
　Willie Masters' Lonesome Wife.
ETIENNE GILSON, *The Arts of the Beautiful.*
　Forms and Substances in the Arts.
C. S. GISCOMBE, *Giscome Road.*
　Here.
　Prairie Style.
DOUGLAS GLOVER, *Bad News of the Heart.*
　The Enamoured Knight.
WITOLD GOMBROWICZ, *A Kind of Testament.*
KAREN ELIZABETH GORDON, *The Red Shoes.*
GEORGI GOSPODINOV, *Natural Novel.*
JUAN GOYTISOLO, *Count Julian.*
　Makbara.
　Marks of Identity.
PATRICK GRAINVILLE, *The Cave of Heaven.*
HENRY GREEN, *Blindness.*
　Concluding.
　Doting.
　Nothing.
JIŘÍ GRUŠA, *The Questionnaire.*
GABRIEL GUDDING, *Rhode Island Notebook.*
JOHN HAWKES, *Whistlejacket.*
AIDAN HIGGINS, *A Bestiary.*
　Bornholm Night-Ferry.
　Flotsam and Jetsam.
　Langrishe, Go Down.
　Scenes from a Receding Past.
　Windy Arbours.
ALDOUS HUXLEY, *Antic Hay.*
　Crome Yellow.
　Point Counter Point.
　Those Barren Leaves.
　Time Must Have a Stop.
MIKHAIL IOSSEL AND JEFF PARKER, EDS., *Amerika:*
　Contemporary Russians View the United States.
GERT JONKE, *Geometric Regional Novel.*
　Homage to Czerny.
JACQUES JOUET, *Mountain R.*
HUGH KENNER, *The Counterfeiters.*
　Flaubert, Joyce and Beckett: The Stoic Comedians.
　Joyce's Voices.
DANILO KIŠ, *Garden, Ashes.*
　A Tomb for Boris Davidovich.
ANITA KONKKA, *A Fool's Paradise.*
GEORGE KONRÁD, *The City Builder.*
TADEUSZ KONWICKI, *A Minor Apocalypse.*
　The Polish Complex.
MENIS KOUMANDAREAS, *Koula.*
ELAINE KRAF, *The Princess of 72nd Street.*
JIM KRUSOE, *Iceland.*
EWA KURYLUK, *Century 21.*
ERIC LAURRENT, *Do Not Touch.*
VIOLETTE LEDUC, *La Bâtarde.*
DEBORAH LEVY, *Billy and Girl.*
　Pillow Talk in Europe and Other Places.
JOSÉ LEZAMA LIMA, *Paradiso.*
ROSA LIKSOM, *Dark Paradise.*
OSMAN LINS, *Avalovara.*
　The Queen of the Prisons of Greece.
ALF MAC LOCHLAINN, *The Corpus in the Library.*
　Out of Focus.
RON LOEWINSOHN, *Magnetic Field(s).*
BRIAN LYNCH, *The Winner of Sorrow.*
D. KEITH MANO, *Take Five.*
MICHELINE AHARONIAN MARCOM, *The Mirror in the Well.*
BEN MARCUS, *The Age of Wire and String.*
WALLACE MARKFIELD, *Teitlebaum's Window.*
　To an Early Grave.
DAVID MARKSON, *Reader's Block.*
　Springer's Progress.
　Wittgenstein's Mistress.
CAROLE MASO, *AVA.*
LADISLAV MATEJKA AND KRYSTYNA POMORSKA, EDS.,
　Readings in Russian Poetics: Formalist and
　Structuralist Views.

HARRY MATHEWS,
The Case of the Persevering Maltese: Collected Essays.
Cigarettes.
The Conversions.
The Human Country: New and Collected Stories.
The Journalist.
My Life in CIA.
Singular Pleasures.
The Sinking of the Odradek Stadium.
Tlooth.
20 Lines a Day.
ROBERT L. McLAUGHLIN, ED.,
Innovations: An Anthology of Modern &
Contemporary Fiction.
HERMAN MELVILLE, *The Confidence-Man.*
AMANDA MICHALOPOULOU, *I'd Like.*
STEVEN MILLHAUSER, *The Barnum Museum.*
In the Penny Arcade.
RALPH J. MILLS, JR., *Essays on Poetry.*
OLIVE MOORE, *Spleen.*
NICHOLAS MOSLEY, *Accident.*
Assassins.
Catastrophe Practice.
Children of Darkness and Light.
Experience and Religion.
The Hesperides Tree.
Hopeful Monsters.
Imago Bird.
Impossible Object.
Inventing God.
Judith.
Look at the Dark.
Natalie Natalia.
Serpent.
Time at War.
The Uses of Slime Mould: Essays of Four Decades.
WARREN MOTTE,
Fables of the Novel: French Fiction since 1990.
Fiction Now: The French Novel in the 21st Century.
Oulipo: A Primer of Potential Literature.
YVES NAVARRE, *Our Share of Time.*
Sweet Tooth.
DOROTHY NELSON, *In Night's City.*
Tar and Feathers.
WILFRIDO D. NOLLEDO, *But for the Lovers.*
FLANN O'BRIEN, *At Swim-Two-Birds.*
At War.
The Best of Myles.
The Dalkey Archive.
Further Cuttings.
The Hard Life.
The Poor Mouth.
The Third Policeman.
CLAUDE OLLIER, *The Mise-en-Scène.*
PATRIK OUŘEDNÍK, *Europeana.*
FERNANDO DEL PASO, *Palinuro of Mexico.*
ROBERT PINGET, *The Inquisitory.*
Mahu or The Material.
Trio.
RAYMOND QUENEAU, *The Last Days.*
Odile.
Pierrot Mon Ami.
Saint Glinglin.
ANN QUIN, *Berg.*
Passages.
Three.
Tripticks.
ISHMAEL REED, *The Free-Lance Pallbearers.*
The Last Days of Louisiana Red.
Reckless Eyeballing.
The Terrible Threes.
The Terrible Twos.
Yellow Back Radio Broke-Down.
JEAN RICARDOU, *Place Names.*
RAINER MARIA RILKE,
The Notebooks of Malte Laurids Brigge.
JULIÁN RÍOS, *Larva: A Midsummer Night's Babel.*
Poundemonium.
AUGUSTO ROA BASTOS, *I the Supreme.*
OLIVIER ROLIN, *Hotel Crystal.*
JACQUES ROUBAUD, *The Great Fire of London.*
Hortense in Exile.
Hortense Is Abducted.
The Plurality of Worlds of Lewis.
The Princess Hoppy.
The Form of a City Changes Faster, Alas,
Than the Human Heart.
Some Thing Black.
LEON S. ROUDIEZ, *French Fiction Revisited.*

VEDRANA RUDAN, *Night.*
LYDIE SALVAYRE, *The Company of Ghosts.*
Everyday Life.
The Lecture.
The Power of Flies.
LUIS RAFAEL SÁNCHEZ, *Macho Camacho's Beat.*
SEVERO SARDUY, *Cobra & Maitreya.*
NATHALIE SARRAUTE, *Do You Hear Them?*
Martereau.
The Planetarium.
ARNO SCHMIDT, *Collected Stories.*
Nobodaddy's Children.
CHRISTINE SCHUTT, *Nightwork.*
GAIL SCOTT, *My Paris.*
JUNE AKERS SEESE,
Is This What Other Women Feel Too?
What Waiting Really Means.
AURELIE SHEEHAN, *Jack Kerouac Is Pregnant.*
VIKTOR SHKLOVSKY, *Knight's Move.*
A Sentimental Journey: Memoirs 1917–1922.
Energy of Delusion: A Book on Plot.
Literature and Cinematography.
Theory of Prose.
Third Factory.
Zoo, or Letters Not about Love.
JOSEF ŠKVORECKÝ,
The Engineer of Human Souls.
CLAUDE SIMON, *The Invitation.*
GILBERT SORRENTINO, *Aberration of Starlight.*
Blue Pastoral.
Crystal Vision.
Imaginative Qualities of Actual Things.
Mulligan Stew.
Pack of Lies.
Red the Fiend.
The Sky Changes.
Something Said.
Splendide-Hôtel.
Steelwork.
Under the Shadow.
W. M. SPACKMAN, *The Complete Fiction.*
GERTRUDE STEIN, *Lucy Church Amiably.*
The Making of Americans.
A Novel of Thank You.
PIOTR SZEWC, *Annihilation.*
STEFAN THEMERSON, *Hobson's Island.*
The Mystery of the Sardine.
Tom Harris.
JEAN-PHILIPPE TOUSSAINT, *The Bathroom.*
Camera.
Monsieur.
Television.
DUMITRU TSEPENEAG, *Pigeon Post.*
Vain Art of the Fugue.
ESTHER TUSQUETS, *Stranded.*
DUBRAVKA UGRESIC, *Lend Me Your Character.*
Thank You for Not Reading.
MATI UNT, *Diary of a Blood Donor.*
Things in the Night.
ÁLVARO URIBE AND OLIVIA SEARS, EDS.,
The Best of Contemporary Mexican Fiction.
ELOY URROZ, *The Obstacles.*
LUISA VALENZUELA, *He Who Searches.*
PAUL VERHAEGHEN, *Omega Minor.*
MARJA-LIISA VARTIO, *The Parson's Widow.*
BORIS VIAN, *Heartsnatcher.*
AUSTRYN WAINHOUSE, *Hedyphagetica.*
PAUL WEST, *Words for a Deaf Daughter & Gala.*
CURTIS WHITE, *America's Magic Mountain.*
The Idea of Home.
Memories of My Father Watching TV.
Monstrous Possibility: An Invitation to
Literary Politics.
Requiem.
DIANE WILLIAMS, *Excitability: Selected Stories.*
Romancer Erector.
DOUGLAS WOOLF, *Wall to Wall.*
Ya! & John-Juan.
JAY WRIGHT, *Polynomials and Pollen.*
The Presentable Art of Reading Absence.
PHILIP WYLIE, *Generation of Vipers.*
MARGUERITE YOUNG, *Angel in the Forest.*
Miss MacIntosh, My Darling.
REYOUNG, *Unbabbling.*
ZORAN ŽIVKOVIĆ, *Hidden Camera.*
LOUIS ZUKOFSKY, *Collected Fiction.*
SCOTT ZWIREN, *God Head.*

FOR A FULL LIST OF PUBLICATIONS, VISIT:
www.dalkeyarchive.com